The Prodigal Son

or

THE SINNER'S RETURN TO GOD

King of Love

"And then come, and accuse me, saith the Lord: If your sins be as scarlet, they shall be made as white as snow: and if they be red as crimson, they shall be white as wool."
—Isaias 1:18

CONTENTS

INTRODUCTORY

The prodigal represents all those who, in the blind pursuit of the riches, pleasures, and honors of this world, have lost sight of the noble end for which God created them, and have forfeited the grace and friendship of Almighty God by mortal sin. The unhappy condition of the prodigal, deprived of all human aid and comfort, represents vividly to our mind the unhappy condition of those who live in the state of mortal sin. The untiring efforts of the prodigal to return to his father's house serve as a model to all those who have abandoned God, and sincerely wish to be received again into the friendship of their Heavenly Father.

INTRODUCTORY.—GOOD READING.

A TRAVELLER once found himself alone on a dreary moor. The ground was covered with snow. The bleak winter wind moaned and blew in fitful gusts. All nature seemed dead around him, and scarcely a star-light gleamed on the dreary tomb. The poor lonely traveller had lost his way. He had been wandering long amid the snow-drifts. He was benumbed with cold, dispirited and weary. Must he lie down upon this bleak moor and die? Must the ice be his bed and the snow his winding-sheet? He thinks of home, but the thought fills his soul with bitterness. Never again shall he feel his fond wife's embrace, never again shall his children welcome him with the merry laugh and the warm, tender kiss. The poor traveller sinks upon the ground in weakness and despair. A distant sound strikes upon his ear, rouses him from his stupor, and fills him with hope. It is the sound of the convent bell ringing the matin chime. The lost traveller shakes off the sleep of death. He sees in the distance a glimmering light. He urges on his weary steps. He reaches the convent door, and is safe.

The state of this unhappy traveller is but a faint image of the unhappy condition of a soul that has strayed from God—from the true faith ; that is wandering about in darkness and doubt, and has sunk into blank despair. At last this unhappy soul reads a pious book. The light of truth flashes upon nis mind. He hastens to the church. He enters her portals, and there finds a peace and contentment oı heart that surpass all understanding. He is saved.

A good book is indeed a faithful friend, that will give us counsel without cowardice or flattery, on the one hand, and without any personal bitterness, on the other. It is alsc one of the best missionaries of the Church. It can enteı places where priests cannot penetrate. A stern hater of the Catholic Church, who on no consideration would hold intercourse with a Catholic priest, will often take a volume of Catholic truth and read it by his fireside.

La Harpe was an infidel and a great friend of Voltaire. He wrote several works against religion. When the French Revolution broke out he was seized and cast into prison. In the silence and solitude of his cell he found time tc examine the truths of religion, which he had hitherto neglected. He tells us how sad and lonely he was in his cell. To while away his time he read a few pious books that had been given him. Gradually the light of faith began to dawn in his heart ; but the heavenly light filled him with terror. All the sins of his life came up before him. He knew that death was at hand ; for in those days there was but one step from the prison to the scaffold. For the first time in forty years he turned to God with an humbled, sorrowful heart, and began to pray. There was no priest near to prepare him for death. They were all either dead or banished. After having offered up a fervent prayer, he opened at random a copy of the *Imitation of Christ* and read these consoling words: "See, my son, I have come to thee because thou hast called me." The words filled him with unspeakable consolation. His heart was touched ; he fell upon his face and burst into tears. This was the beginning of a new life. La Harpe was afterwards set free ; but he remained ever after faithful to the good resolutions he had formed whilst shut up in his dreary prison.

Dr. Palafox, the pious Bishop of Osma, in his preface to the letters of St. Teresa, relates that an eminent Lutheran minister at Bremen, who was famed for several works which he had published against the Catholic Church, purchased the *Life of St. Teresa,* with a view of attempting to confute it. But after reading it over attentively, he was converted to the Catholic faith, and from that time forward led a most edifying life.

A thousand such examples might be offered to show that the reading of pious books is well calculated to lead sinners to a life of grace, and to encourage the just to walk steadily onward on the road to perfection. The tendency of pious reading to induce men of the world to change their ways and enter on the path of a holy life, may be seen from the conversion of St. Augustine. The extreme repugnance which, previous to his conversion, the saint felt in his soul at the thought of parting with the false pleasures of sense and surrendering himself in full to the service of Christ, is well known to readers of his life. What a terrible conflict, what fierce attacks, he experienced within his heart! The story of the conflict, as told by himself, moves us to pity. He tells us that he groaned as he felt his own will, like a heavy chain, holding him fast; and that the enemy of man kept even his power of willing shackled by a kind of cruel necessity. He went through an agony of death in ridding himself of his vicious habits. When just on the point of resolving to renounce them, the old fascinations and false delights dragged him back, and he heard low voices murmur, "Do you mean to forsake us? From this moment forth are we never, never more to be with you?" But what was it that finally, after so fierce a struggle, overcame the heart of the saint? What won that heroic soul to God? The final victory was due to the reading of a pious book. To this is to be attributed, under Almighty God, the glory of gaining to the Church so renowned a doctor and saint. It

9

happened that whilst Augustine was fighting with the wild thoughts that filled his breast, he heard a voice saying to him, " Take and read " He obeyed the voice ; and taking up a book which lay near him, read a chapter from St. Paul Shortly after the dark clouds passed away from his mind, the hardness of his heart yielded, and peace and calm took possession of his soul, where before tumultuous passions and despair were striving for the mastery. The chains of his bad habits were broken ; he gave himself up without reserve to God, and became the great saint who is admired by all the world, and revered upon the altars of the Church.

CHAPTER I.

ON arriving in the strange country the prodigal plunged immediately into bad company. He passed his time and squandered his money among those lost creatures—the disgrace of their sex—whose life is dishonor and whose end is eternal torments. "This thy son hath devoured his substance with harlots." * Alas! the prodigal has many followers. Every one who likes to associate with the impure will soon be infected with their impurities.

"Evil communications corrupt good manners." Why is it that the association with the wicked corrupts our manners and our morals? We meet a wicked man; we hold intercourse with him, and are never after what we were before. We feel that something has gone forth from him and entered into our life, so that we are not, and can never be again, the man we were before we met him. What is the explanation of this fact? How happens it that we are benefited by intercourse with the good, and injured by intercourse with the bad? How is it that one man is able to influence another, whether for good or for evil? What is the meaning of influence itself? Influence—inflowing, flowing in. What is this but the fact that man is a being whose life is dependent on an exterior object? God alone can live in, from, and by Himself, uninfluenced and unaffected by anything distinguishable from His own being. But man is not God. He is a dependent being, yet free to choose good

* Luke xv. 80

11

or evil; to side with God or with the devil; to follow truth or falsehood, light or darkness; to embrace virtue or vice. In consequence of the fall of Adam, he feels more inclined for evil than for good. Baptism, indeed, cancels original sin in our soul, but it does not destroy our natural inclination to evil, which we have inherited from our first parents. The great Apostle St. Paul bears witness to this when he says : "I do not that good which I will, but the evil which I hate, that I do." * That is to say, I do not wish to do evil; I even try to avoid it; but I experience within myself a continual inclination to evil; I endeavor to do good, but I feel within myself a great reluctance thereto, and I must do violence to myself in order to act aright. Every one has from his childhood experienced this evil inclination. We naturally feel more inclined to anger than to meekness, to disobedience than to submission; we are more prone to hatred than to love; more inclined to gratify the evil desires of our heart than to practise the holy virtue of purity; we prefer our own ease to visiting Jesus Christ in the Blessed Sacrament, or receiving Him in the Holy Communion. We are naturally indifferent toward God and His religion; we lack fervor in His divine service; we often feel more inclined to join a forbidden society than to enter a pious confraternity; we often find more pleasure in reading a bad or useless book than one that is good and edifying; we are more apt to listen to uncharitable and unbecoming conversation than to the word of God; we feel naturally more inclined to vain-glory, pride, and levity, than to humility, self-control, and the spirit of mortification.

Now, when we place ourselves wilfully under circumstances in which this natural inclination to evil is nourished, so strong does the inclination become that it is morally impossible to resist it. Charles, King of Navarre, was once affected with great weakness of the nerves. By order of the

* Rom. vii. 14.

physician he was sewed up in cloths moistened with brandy, in order that by this strengthening stimulant his cool nerves might be heated and his drooping spirits raised. But the attendant who sewed the cloths unfortunately burned off the thread with a candle, and the linen took fire with such fury that there was no means of saving the poor prince. In a few moments he was but a cinder. We must bear in mind that our soul is wrapped up in weak flesh, as in a cloth, not moistened with brandy, but with something a thousand times more inflammable—with the passion of lust. If we bring our soul too near the fire of sinful occasions, it will immediately take fire. The very presence, the very sight, of that person for whom passion is felt, has a fascinating power. A moment's conversation, a single word, a look, a gesture, casts a spark of impure fire into the innocent soul; and that fire is soon fanned into a fierce flame that may never be extinguished. There are some who say that the sin of impurity is but a small evil, a human weakness. But who are those who say so? Ah! it is only the impure, the unchaste.

The law of nature, written in every man's heart—the voice of conscience—tells him that it is a sin to defile his soul and body by the shameful vice of impurity. Every one is born with a natural sense of modesty. A certain feeling of shame restrains the heart, as yet unsullied, from every thought, word, and action. The honest blood rushes from the pure heart and mantles the flushing cheek whenever anything immodest is spoken of or hinted at. The voice of conscience warns every one before he commits the shameful deed. And when at last, after long and fearful struggles, a pure man has unhappily consented to sin, his feelings of shame, of agony, and remorse torture and crucify him.

Where is the man who does not feel and know for certain that the vice of impurity defiles and dishonors him? Where

13

is the man who, after having committed the foul deed, does not feel degraded in his own eyes—whose conscience does not torture and reproach him? Where is the man who, after having gratified his vile passion, does not feel how empty and drear his heart is—how poor and wretched this sin has made him?

The libertine seeks the most secret nook, the darkest night, to cover and conceal his infamy. He strives to hide the blush of shame beneath the fall of darkness and secrecy. He whispers into the ear of his unhappy victim, "No one sees us;" but he forgets that there is an Eye that sees all, that there is One before whom the darkest night is as the broad light of day. Why does he act thus? It is because his own conscience condemns his foul actions.

Among the old heathen tribes in Germany and Gaul, if a young girl lost her innocence, her father had the power to put her to death, and thus wash away the stain of dishonor from his family. St. Boniface tells us, in his letter to King Ethelbald of Mercia, that it was a custom and law among the Saxons that if a girl dishonored her family or a woman proved faithless to her husband, the unhappy wretch was forced to take a rope and hang herself. Her infamous body was then cut down and burned. The villain that had ruined the unhappy creature was then dragged to the spot and hanged like a dog over the smoking ashes of her whom he had ruined. In other places, whenever a woman fell into sin, all the women of the place gathered around the guilty one, drove her from place to place, and scourged her till at last she fell bleeding and exhausted to the ground.

Another ancient law decrees that "if a woman prove faithless to her husband, both she and her seducer shall be dragged to the place of execution. There a grave is dug seven feet long and seven feet deep, and filled with sharp thorns. The guilty pair are tied together and hurled into the grave. A long, sharp stake is then driven through their

14

yet living bodies, the earth is then heaped over them, and they are left there to perish."

Why is it that we find even among the heathens such severe punishments inflicted upon the impure? It is because they knew by the light of reason how heinous and shameful a crime the sin of impurity was.

What is it that gives the young man, and especially the young woman, their freshness, their beauty, their loveliness? Is it not innocence, purity of heart, stainless virginity? This heavenly virtue casts around them a halo of glory that nothing else can give.

But if this lustre is once lost, if the lily of purity once withers and dies, what can replace it? That young woman, with all her beauty, with all her finery, is but an ornamented corpse, a gilded tomb wreathed with flowers; without all fair, but within full of mould and stench and rottenness. Of what avail are all her ornaments, her silks and satins, her gold and precious stones, if she has lost the greatest ornament of all—her virtue? All these are but the symbols, the fit ornaments, of a chaste and noble heart. On those who have lost their innocence they are but a glaring mockery, the sad remembrance of what their wearer once was and might have been. Away, then, with costly trappings — the price, perhaps, of lost honor; they are but the flimsy tinsel that covers a vile and degraded heart.

"Your bodies," says St. Paul, "are the living temples of the Holy Ghost." What a crime it is to profane the church, to dishonor the sacred chalice or ciborium! But how much more enormous is the sin of a Christian who dishonors his soul and body by the sin of impurity! If it be a sacrilege to profane the material temple of God, the lifeless vases consecrated to his service, how much greater is the crime of him who profanes the living temple of God; how much greater is the crime of him who defiles his soul

15

and body, which are consecrated to God by the most inti mate union with Him !

Let us be mindful of our dignity. Our soul was made the image of God in creation and to the likeness of God in baptism. The vice of impurity especially defiles and dishonors the soul and degrades it to the likeness of the brute. "Your bodies," says St. Paul, "are members of the body of Christ."* Your body has become intimately united with Jesus Christ in baptism, but more especially in Holy Communion. You can say with truth, especially after having received Holy Communion, that the blood of a God flows in your veins. What an unspeakable honor ! Men boast of their ancestry. They are proud of royal blood and the blood of heroes. How great, then, is the honor of a Christian in whose veins flows the blood of the King of kings—the blood of God ! What a burning shame, then, what a horrible sacrilege, is it for a Christian to defile his body and soul by the foul vice of impurity ! By committing that sin he dishonors Jesus Christ. He causes Jesus, the God of purity, to serve him in his sins. He takes the members of the body of Jesus Christ, as the Apostle assures us, and makes of them the members of a harlot.* This crime, as St. Paul the Apostle assures us, is so great that it should not be even named among Christians. Now, if it be forbidden even to name this sin, what must it be to commit it ? " Do not err," says St. Paul : " neither fornicators, nor adulterers, nor the effeminate shall possess the kingdom of God."† "Whatsoever sin you name," says St. Isidore, " you shall find nothing equal to this crime."‡ Indeed, " There is nothing more vile or degrading," says St. Jerome, " than to allow one's self to be conquered by the flesh." In the lives of the ancient Fathers it is related § that a certain hermit, being once favored with the company of an angel, met on his way the fetid carcass of a dog. The angel gave no sign of

* 1 Cor. vi. 15.   † 1 Cor. vi. 9.   ‡ Tom. Orat. xxi.   § Part ii. c. viii.

displeasure at the smell which it exhaled. They afterwards met a young man elegantly dressed and highly perfumed. The angel stopped his nostrils. Being asked by the hermit why he did so, he answered that the young man, on account of the vice of impurity in which he indulged, sent forth a far more intolerable stench than the putrid dog which they had passed.

"In no sin," says St. Thomas, "does the devil delight so much as in sins against chastity" (i. ii. q. 73, a. 3). The reason why the devil takes so much delight in this vice is because it is difficult for a person who is addicted to it to be delivered from it. And why? Because this sin so blinds the sinner that he commits it oftener than any other sin. A blasphemer only blasphemes when he is drunk or provoked to anger. The assassin, whose trade is to murder others, does not, at the most, commit more than eight or ten homicides. But the unchaste are guilty of an unceasing torrent of sins, by thoughts, by words, by looks, by complacencies, and by touches, so that when they go to confession they find it impossible to tell the number of sins they have committed against chastity. Even in their sleep the devil represents to them obscene objects, that on awakening they may take delight in them; and, being the slaves of the devil, they obey him, and give consent to his evil suggestions. "There is," says St. Thomas, "no sinner so ready to offend God as the votary of lust is" on every occasion that occurs to him. To other sins, such as blasphemy murder, and slander, men are not prone; but to this vice of impurity nature inclines them, and therefore it is so easy to contract the habit. How many foundlings, abortions, infanticides, may one count every day in our large cities! How few young couples come with pure hearts to the altar! How many lost creatures earn a livelihood by a life of infamy! How many houses of shame! How many so-called fashionable houses of assignation in every city—houses of

17

infamy not only for hoary sinners, but even for young and thoughtless children !

What forms the favorite topic of conversation in company, in the cars, on the boats, in the tavern, in the streets, in the market-place, in the ball-room, in the theatre ? Is it not the shameful vice of impurity ?

What constitutes the interest of the great majority of the novels, magazines, weeklies, that fill our libraries, that are to be found in the hands of every one from the young school miss to the venerable old maid ? Is it not sensual love ? Is it not impurity ?

Which dances are the most popular ? Are not the obscene, impure round dances ? How many a young girl will tell you that she will not give up these forbidden dances, even if she had to burn in hell for it !

Which are the most popular plays in the theatre ? What plays are those that always draw crowded houses, while the churches are often empty ? Are they not the most immodest plays that hell itself could invent—plays wherein lost creatures sell their modesty to make a paltry living ?

What class of pictures is to be found in those weekly papers ? What kind of photographs and statues in the windows of so many stores ? Are they not usually the most indecent ?

Another reason why the devil delights so much in seeing men commit the sin of impurity is that it is the fruitful source of so many other sins. The impure man is, to a certain degree, guilty of idolatry—of giving to some creature the love and honor which are due to God alone.

Is not that impure man guilty of idolatry who loves the frail, erring creature of his passion to such a degree that for her sake he willingly sacrifices his health, his honor, his hope of heaven, and God Himself ? Does he not love that creature more than God ? And is not that idolatry ?

The impure man is guilty of perjury. Impurity leads to

perjury. Is not the young woman who protests solemnly to her parents that she keeps no dangerous company; is not that vain woman who protests again and again to her husband that she receives no dangerous visits, guilty of perjury when they call God to bear witness to their innocence, though they know in their inmost hearts that they are not innocent? How many false oaths has not that young man taken; how often has he solemnly sworn to the unhappy victim of his passion that he would never abandon her; and how quickly has that solemn promise been broken as soon as his brutal passions were gratified!

Impurity leads to sacrilege. Who are those that make bad confessions? Who are those that conceal their sins in confession, and make so many sacrilegious communions? They are, in every case almost, those who have been guilty of the crime of impurity. They are ashamed to confess their secret crimes. They will not reveal to their confessor the dangerous company they keep, the sinful liberties they permit, the shameful thoughts and desires that they nourish in their hearts. They never mention to the confessor the wicked books that they read, the immodest conversation in which they indulge. And even if they do mention any sin of this kind, they never tell the whole truth; they cover and lessen the sin; so that their confession is worthless, and they leave the confessional with the curse of God and the sin of sacrilege on their soul. Oh! how many of these souls are lost for ever. How many are now burning in hell who were led astray by the demon of impurity, and who afterwards had not the courage to open their hearts sincerely, to tell everything honestly to their confessor!

Impurity leads to theft. A young man filches from his employer; he keeps back part of his wages, that he may have the means to spend the night in those haunts of sin and shame which are the very hot-beds of hell. The young woman steals from her parents in order to buy some finery which she thinks will make her more captivating in the eyes of others. A husband and a father squanders his means and ruins his family in order to gratify the vanity of some infamous woman who has gained those affections which alone belong to his lawful wife. To gratify his passion he is even cruel to his family.

A certain man kept a mistress in the house. His wife knew it, but bore the insult patiently, in order to prevent greater evils. One day, the servant came to this good lady with tears in her eyes. "What is the matter? Why do you weep?" asked the good woman. "Ah!" answered the servant, "your husband has sent me to take the keys of the house from you. He says that henceforth this young woman in the house is to be my mistress." The lady grew pale, her heart pierced by this last crowning insult, went to the "mistress," and ordered her to quit the house instantly. The husband heard of the difficulty. He told his wife if she did not beg pardon on her knees of the mistress, he would send her and her child a thousand miles away, where she would never see him again. And the poor mother had to obey.

Impurity leads to cruelty and hardness of heart. There lived some years ago in the city of Vienna a young widow. She had an only child—a little girl of about six years of age, named Lena. Soon after the death of her husband, this young widow began to receive the visits of a young man of the neighborhood. By and by the visits became more frequent, their friendship ripened into intimacy, and wicked tongues were not wanting to whisper suspicions that this innocent friendship would end in shame. The young widow felt the shame of her unhappy position very keenly; but she was blinded by her passions, and would not give up the young man's company. She urged him frequently to save her from shame by an honorable marriage; but he steadily refused "I cannot marry a woman with a fam ily," he said ; "it would only bring trouble." At last the woman, who had now given herself up entirely to the devil, formed the horrible resolution to do away with her child, and thus set aside every obstacle to the wished-for union. In the house in which she lived there was a deep, dark cellar. One day the unhappy woman took her little daughter by the hand, led her down into this damp, gloomy dungeon, and said, in a harsh tone : " Here, Lena, remain here until I come back for you." The poor innocent child began to cry, but the unnatural mother hurried away, and closed the heavy door behind her. Two days passed. The mother hoped now that her little child was dead. In the darkness of the night she stole down to the cellar, slowly opened the door, and called out : " Lena, are you there ? " The sad, plaintive voice of the little child was heard : " Ah ! mamma, mamma, give me a piece of bread." But the mother turned away and closed the heavy door once more. Another day passed by. The mother spent it in the company of her wicked companion, gratifying her sinful passions ; and the poor helpless child remained pining away with hunger in her gloomy prison. Once more the wretched woman went down to the cellar. This time she expected for certain that the child would be dead. She opened the door and called again, " Lena, are you there ? " Again the sad, moaning voice of her child was heard, crying in feeble tones : " O mamma, mamma ! a piece of bread." The unnatural mother turned away ; her heart trembled not with compassion—the impure heart has no compassion—but with fear lest she should be found out. She trembled with rage that her child was not yet dead. She now waited several days, and when she went to the cellar once more, the child was dead ! She took the poor dead child to her room and dressed it for burial. Early the next morning the neighbors were aroused by loud wailing and lamenting in the house of the young widow. They hastened to her room ;

they found her crying and shrieking and acting as if she were beside herself with grief. There lay the dead child, pale and cold. It was dressed in white ; a wreath of flowers was placed upon its breast. No one suspected anything of the foul, unnatural murder. Next day the child was buried. All the little playmates of Lena formed a procession and accompanied the body to the grave. The body of the dead child was now lowered into the grave ; the first handful of earth was thrown upon the coffin ; the priest then knelt down with all those present, and recited the customary prayers. Every heart was touched—every eye filled with tears. There was one heart, however, that remained cold and unmoved ; it was the heart of the mother. She was now free. She could now gratify her sinful passions without restraint; there was no longer any fear of detection. The secret deed was locked up securely in her heart. But oh ! terrible justice of God ! when the priest recited the " Our Father," and came to the words, " Give us this day our daily bread," the sad, plaintive cry of her dying child rang in the ears of the mother ; a wild feeling of terror and remorse seized her, and she fell senseless to the ground. She came to herself again, but she had lost her reason and become a raving maniac. And now, with a wild, unearthly laugh, she related to the horror-stricken bystanders the full particulars of the murder of her child.

Impurity leads to jealousy, murder, and suicide. George Bauman, one of the principals of the Public Schools of Williamsburg, N. Y., and Annie McNamara, both Catholics, met frequently for nine months in a house of assignation in Elizabeth Street, in New York. Bauman at last shot her, and then shot himself, in that infamous house. Their bodies were taken to the Morgue near Bellevue Hospital, where they were laid out in coffins side by side. The face of the unhappy murderer looked as if he had died in the most terrible agony.

22

About four years ago, Catherine Lenan, a virtuous and handsome young girl, left her home in the County Cork and came to this country, where she soon obtained employment as a domestic servant; her last place being in Longwood, near Brookline, Mass. She was a careful and industrious girl, and those who employed her became attached to her. There were few or none of those near her whom she had known in Ireland; she had only one relative in this country, who lived at a distance from her. Thrown upon herself, she naturally wanted to form new acquaintances and make new friends; and we soon find her, in company with another girl, walking from her employer's house on every evening she could spare, and visiting a saloon or drinking-house, kept by Irish people, where she had become acquainted with several young men. In taking this walk on the night of Tuesday, Oct. 24, poor Kate Lenan was waylaid on the road by some miscreant yet unknown, and brutally outraged and murdered!

The third reason why the devil takes peculiar delight in the vice of impurity is because this sin involves the malice of scandal. Other sins, such as blasphemy, perjury, and murder, excite horror in those who witness them; but this sin easily excites and draws others to commit it, or at least to commit it with less horror. Ignorance of evil is a part of innocence, and the best rampart of virtue. Those who have never seen evil done think not of seeing it. They will entertain a horror of it unless they see it committed and excused by others. One is ashamed to practise virtue among the wicked, and to be innocent among the guilty. How many have received their first lessons in immorality or crime from the hostler, or the cook, or the nurse; while a single night with a strange bedfellow may initiate a boy in mysteries to which he had else remained a stranger. This last danger is greatly increased if the casual room-mate be by a few years his senior; for the power of mischief possessed by the older boy is increased in proportion to his size and his experience. An impure boy or girl is sure to corrupt the smaller ones whenever a safe opportunity presents itself, and thus children of six and twelve fall victims to those who are older than themselves.

The fourth reason why the devil rejoices so much in seeing one commit the sin of impurity, is because it blinds the sinner to such an extent as not to allow him to see the injury which he offers to God, nor the miserable state in which he lives and sleeps. Like " the sow wallowing in the mire," the impure are immersed in their own filth, so that they are not sensible of the malice of their actions, and therefore they neither feel nor abhor the stench of their impurities, which excite disgust and horror in all others. By this sin they lose the light of God, which shines in the hearts of all his children, so that they may not stray from the narrow path that leads to heaven. But suddenly this light of the soul is extinguished by the sin of impurity, and the impure are left in utter darkness. Their sins degrade and dim their understanding more than does any other vice. They have eyes and see not, they have ears and hear not, they have reason and understand not. If the unchaste are deprived of light, and no longer see the evil which they do, how can they detest it and amend their lives ? The prophet says that, being blinded by their own mire, they do not even think of returning to God. Their impurities take away from them all knowledge of God. " They will not set their thoughts to return to their God, for the spirit of fornication is in the midst of them, and they have not known the Lord." * Yes, this sin, if often repeated, will become a habit, and this habit will become so strengthened and deeply rooted in the soul by repeated falls till it finally attains to a degree of malice that is truly devilish.

Whoever has arrived at this degree of sin is possessed by

* Osee v. 4

a hardened, unyielding determination to commit sin—a determination which neither warnings nor threats, neither punishments nor favors, can change. Shrouded in impenetrable darkness, in insolent defiance of God and man, the rays of divine light cannot penetrate this heart. The unhappy man is separated from God. The wounds of his conscience have become encrusted so that he can no longer feel any remorse, and at last he reaches such a depth of wickedness that it is almost impossible for him to become either better or worse.

By lust the devil triumphs over the entire man—over his body and over his soul—over his memory, by filling it with unchaste thoughts and making him take pleasure in them; over his intellect, by making him desire occasions of committing sin; over his will, by making it love its impurities as his last end, and as if there were no God. Hell governs him, hell dwells in him; he is already, one may say, a victim doomed to the flames, an agent and slave of the devil. What Jesus said of Judas may be said of him: "One of you is a devil. There is one among you, and it were better for him that he had never been born."

A certain person was so much addicted to the vice of impurity as to commit the most atrocious crimes no longer through weakness, but out of sheer hatred of God. Her accomplice died suddenly in the very act of a most abominable sin of impurity, and afterwards appeared to her enveloped in fire and flames. From that time forward she felt within her, as it were, a burning so intense that she imagined herself in hell, and kept uttering the most horrible cries of despair. This happened in 1858 in a city of Pennsylvania.

There stood once in the middle of Jerusalem a beautiful temple. It was adorned with silver, and gold, and precious stones. It was the work of many kings, and the wonder of ages. In an unhappy hour a torch was cast by a soldier's hand into this beautiful temple. It caught fire, the flames gained apace, and soon the glorious temple was a heap of smoldering ruins. Jews and Romans, the friends and the stranger, made every effort to save the temple, but their efforts were of no avail.

What a sad image this temple is of the soul that has been ruined by the vice of impurity ! A single spark of impure fire is cast into the pure soul which is the temple of the living God. The spark is soon fanned into a flame—the hellish flame increases and gains full mastery over the soul— the friends and relations of the deluded creature may speak to her—the priest of God may warn her—heaven and earth may strive to save her ; but in vain. The impure fire, the flame of impure love, burns on—it burns to the very verge of the grave, to the very brink of hell, where the worm never dieth and the fire never quenches.

This vice when habitual clings so firmly to nature that the desire for carnal pleasures becomes insatiable, and will cease only when the unhappy man who indulges in it is cast into the fire of hell. "O hellish fire !—lust, whose fuel is gluttony, whose sparks are brief conversations, whose end is hell." The unchaste become like the vulture that waits to be killed by the fowler, rather than abandon the rotten-ness of the dead bodies on which it feeds.

Some years ago a gentleman of rank and education forgot himself so far as to keep in his house a young woman of loose character. His friends, his relatives, and even the priest of God, advised and begged him again and again to give up that wicked girl. But it was all in vain. His only answer was : I cannot, I cannot. At last he fell sick, and his illness became so dangerous that he was at the point of death. The good priest now came to see him. He saluted the dying man, and spoke kindly to him, in order to win his confidence. "My dear friend," said the priest, "your illness is dangerous, it is true, but you are young yet, you have a strong constitution, and we hope that you will recover.

But, at all events, it would do you no harm to make your peace with God like a good Christian." "Ah! father," said the dying man, "I know that I am in great danger. It is true, I have led a very wicked life, but I now wish to amend. I wish to die a good death. Tell me, then, what I must do." The priest was overjoyed to see him in such a good disposition. "Well," said the priest, "since you desire to die a good death, you must prepare yourself by a good confession." "Oh! most willingly," was the reply. "Are there any debts that you have not paid?" asked the priest before he commenced to hear his confession. "I have paid them all," answered the sick man. "Have you never defrauded your neighbor or injured him in his good name or property?" "Yes, but I have made restitution." "Have you no ill-will against any of your neighbors?" "I had, but I have forgiven them all." "Are you willing to ask pardon of all those whom you may have offended?" "Yes, I humbly ask pardon." "Do you wish, then, to receive the last sacraments?" "I desire it with all my heart." "Well, then," said the priest, "since you desire to receive the last sacraments, you know you must put away every obstacle to the grace of God—you must send away this wicked girl from your house; she is a constant occasion of sin to you still. You must send her away." "O father!" said the dying man, "what do you mean? Send away that girl! Oh! I cannot do that." "What is that?" said the priest, amazed. "You cannot. Why can you not? Do you not know that you must do so if you wish to save your soul?" "Father, I cannot, I cannot." "But you are at the point of death. In a few moments more you will be forced to leave her. Why not send her away now of your own free will?" "I cannot do it, indeed I cannot." "Oh!" cried the priest, drawing forth his crucifix, "look at this crucifix. Our Redeemer, your Lord, suffered and died for you. He shed His heart's blood for you. Will you not make this slight sacrifice to please Him? Oh! look upon His wounds; see His blessed head crowned with thorns—can you refuse him? For the love of Jesus, have pity on your poor soul. Will you not send away that wicked woman, at least for the love of Jesus Christ?" "Father, I have told you already that I cannot do it." "But if you do not send her away, I cannot give you the sacraments." "No matter, I cannot do it." "You will be excluded from the kingdom of heaven." "Well, I cannot help it." "You will die excommunicated; you cannot be buried in consecrated ground, you will be thrown aside like a dog, or an abortion!" "I cannot help it." "But you will be condemned to the everlasting flames of hell." "Well, I cannot help it." "In the name of God, be reasonable. Is it not better to send away this wicked woman than to lose soul and body, heaven, and God Himself?" "I cannot send her away." The dying man then beckoned to the wretched woman, who was standing at some distance from him, and wept. As soon as she drew near, he threw his arms around her neck, and, in a voice which trembled with weakness and passion, he cried: "Ah! you have been my joy during life, you shall be my joy in death and throughout all eternity." These were his last words. In that same instant he breathed forth his soul, and died in the very act of sin.

Oh! how difficult it is for a person who has contracted the habit of this vice to amend his life and return sincerely to God! How difficult it is for him not to put an end to this habit in hell, like the unfortunate man of whom I have just spoken.

During the late war, a young man, a soldier in the hospital at New Berne, was reduced to a skeleton from the excess of impurity. He was lying in his agony for three days, and yet all the time he was seen committing self-abuse. Two other young soldiers in New Berne killed themselves by the excess of this accursed vice. The impure labor un-

28

der another illusion. They say that God has compassion on
this sin. Has he? God has chastised no vice so severely
as the vice of impurity. Read the Scriptures, and you
will find that in punishment of this sin God sent fire from
heaven, and in an instant burnt five cities, with all their inhabitants, nay, even the very stones of these cities. "And
the Lord rained upon Sodom and Gomorrha brimstone and
fire from the Lord out of heaven. And he destroyed these
cities, and all things that spring from the earth."* In
punishment of the sin of impurity, God sent on the earth
the universal deluge, in which the whole human race per-
ished with the exception of eight persons. We also read in
the Scriptures that the Hebrews, having entered Settim, a
city of the Moabites, fell into sin with the women of the
place. In punishment for their sins, God ordered Moses to
put twenty-four thousand of the Hebrews to the sword.†

At the present day, we see more severe temporal punishments inflicted on this than on any other sin. Go into the
hospitals, and listen to the shrieks of so many young persons of both sexes. Ask them why they are obliged to
submit to the severest treatment and to the most painful
operations, and they will tell you that it is on account of
the sins of impurity. At the first glance, the impure man
presents an aspect of languor, weakness, and thinness.
His countenance is pale, sunken, flabby, often leaden, or
more or less livid, with a dark circle around the sunken
eyes, which are dull, and lowered or averted. His physi-
ognomy is sad and spiritless; his voice feeble and hoarse.
There are dry cough, oppression, panting and fatigue on
the least exertion; palpitations, dimness of sight, dizziness,
trembling, painful cramps, convulsive movements like epi-
lepsy; pains in the limbs or at the back of the head, in the
spine, breast, or stomach; great weakness in the back;
sometimes lethargy; at other times slow, consumptive

fever, digestive derangements, nausea, vomiting, loss of appetite, or progressive emaciation. Sometimes the body is bent, and often there are all the appearances of pulmonary consumption, or the characteristics of decrepitude joined to the habits and pretensions of youth. What a wretched and degraded being such a man becomes! He bends under the weight of his crime and infamy, dragging in darkness a remnant of material and animal life. Unhappy man! He has sinned against God, against nature, against himself. He has violated the laws of the Creator. He has disfigured the image of God in his own person, and has changed it into that of the beast. He has sunk lower than the brute, and, like the brute, looks only upon the ground. His dull and stupid glance can no longer raise itself toward heaven. He no longer dares to lift his brow, already stamped with the seal of reprobation. He descends little by little into death, and a last convulsive crisis comes at length, violently to close this strange and horrible drama. (Dr. Debreyne.)

But while the physical symptoms are so grave, the moral degradation goes even further. The impure man, the desecrator of his own body, gradually loses his moral faculties; he becomes dull, silly, listless, embarrassed, sad, effeminate, in his exterior; he becomes indolent, averse to and incapable of all intellectual exertion; he is destitute of all presence of mind ; he is discountenanced, troubled, inquiet, whenever he finds himself in company ; he is taken by surprise and even alarmed if required simply to reply to a child's question; his feeble soul succumbs to the lightest task ; his memory daily losing more and more, he is unable to comprehend the most common things, or to connect the simplest ideas. The greatest means and the brightest talents are soon exhausted ; knowledge previously acquired is forgotten; the most exquisite intelligence becomes naught. and no longer bears fruit ; all the vivacity, all the pride,

all the qualities of the spirit disappear; the power of the
imagination is at an end for them; pleasure no longer
fawns upon them ; but, in revenge, all that is trouble and
misfortune in the world seems the portion of the impure
fellow. Inquietude, dismay, fear, which are his only affections, banish every agreeable sensation from his mind
The last crisis of melancholy and the most frightful suggestions of despair commonly end in hastening the death of
the unfortunate man, or else he falls into complete apathy,
and sinks below those brutes which have the least instinct,
retaining only the figure of his race. It even frequently
happens that the most complete folly and frenzy are manifest from the first. (Dr. Gottlieb Wogel.)

One day a young man spoke to me about one of his companions who had lost his mind. I told him that many young
men nowadays lose their minds on account of self-abuse.
He then avowed that he, too, had lost his mind for some
time, and was taken to the mad-house ; God permitted him
to recover his mind that he might repent. But he soon
after relapsed and was again taken to the mad-house. The
overseer told one of my friends that two-thirds of the inmates lost their minds through the shameful sin of self-
abuse. Such, then, is the physical degradation of the impure man—of the desecrator of his own body. If these evils
are not always visible, yet they are all present, and will show
themselves in proportion as the vice of impurity is practised.

Not all offenders, it is true, are visited so severely as above
described. Perhaps even a small proportion of the whole
number die in this manner ; yet in this comparatively small
minority those who persist in the practice will, sooner or
later, surely be included. Let no one delude himself with
the false assumption that he can be exempt from this universal law. There can be no possible exemption. Those
who persist will surely die the death most horrible of all

31

deaths ; while the very individuals who seem to escape are those who most surely carry their punishment for the remainder of their lives, never live to attain old age, and frequently fall victims to some chronic disease, the germs of which they owe to this detestable vice. "Thou hast cast me off behind thy back," says the Lord ; "bear thou also thy wickedness and thy fornications."*

Doctor Tissot relates that a young man from Montpelier, a student of medicine, died from excess of the crime of impurity. The idea of his crime so agitated his mind that he died in a kind of despair, believing that he saw hell open at his side to receive him.

L. D., a watchmaker, had been virtuous and healthy until the age of seventeen. At that time he delivered himself to the vice of impurity, which he committed three times a day. In less than one year he began to experience great weakness after each criminal act. This warning was not sufficient to drive him from the danger. His soul, already wholly delivered to sin, was no longer capable of other ideas, and the repetition of the crime became every day more frequent, until he found himself in a condition which led him to be apprehensive of death. Wise too late, the evil had made such progress that he could not be cured. He soon suffered from habitual spasms, which often seized him without apparent cause, and in so violent a manner that, during the paroxysm, which sometimes lasted fifteen hours, and never less than eight, he experienced in the back of the neck such violent pains that he commonly raised, not cries merely, but howls, and it was impossible for him, during all this time, to swallow either liquids or solids. His voice became hoarse ; he entirely lost his strength. Obliged to abandon his profession, overwhelmed with misery, he languished almost without relief for several months. A trace of memory, which had nearly vanished, only served to remind him in

* Ezech. xxiii. 35.

cessantly of the causes of his misfortune and to increase his remorse. He was less a living being than a corpse, groaning upon the straw, emaciated, pale, filthy, exhaling an infectious odor, almost incapable of any movement. Often a pale and watery blood issued from the nose, and a constant slime flowed from the mouth. Like a pig, he wallowed in his own abominable filth. Bleared, troubled, and dull, he had no longer the faculty of motion. His pulse was extremely low and rapid ; his breathing very difficult ; his emaciation excessive, except at the feet, which commenced to become dropsical. The disorder of his mind was just as frightful. Without memory ; incapable of connecting two phrases ; without reflection ; without inquietude as to his fate ; with no other sentiment than that of pain ; a being far below the brute ; a spectacle of which it is impossible to conceive the horror, one would with difficulty recognize that he had formerly belonged to the human species. He died at the end of some weeks (June 17, 1857), dropsical from head to foot.

Two young Spaniards, Ferdinand and Alonso, lived at Madrid. They were friends, of respectable family, and led very immoral lives. One night Ferdinand had a dream or vision. On a sudden the door of his chamber flew open. Two enormous giants, black and hideous, rushed towards him, seized and carried him with incredible swiftness to the shore of the sea. The night was a fearful one, dark and stormy. The wind howled wildly around him ; the foaming waves were lashed into fury and rose to an immense height. His ears were stunned by the deafening peals of thunder, and his eyes blinded by the vivid flashes of lightning, which one moment lit up everything with fearful brilliancy, and then again left everything in utter darkness. By the gleam of the lightning, he noticed a vast multitude of persons standing on the shore. A number of phantom ships were sailing swiftly towards him, and to his horror he saw that

33

they were swarming with ghostly spectres, who hurried to and fro with wild, unearthly yells. The ships reached the shore. The demons seized and bound with chains every one they could find, and carried them quickly to their vessels. Among the prisoners, Ferdinand noticed his friend Alonso. In a moment, the grim spectres surrounded himself, seized him, and were carrying him away, when, in an agony of terror, he called aloud upon the sweet names of Jesus and Mary, and suddenly the frightful vision vanished. Ferdinand now found himself transported before the judgment-seat of God. Jesus Christ, the Eternal Judge, was seated on His throne, surrounded by myriads of angels. On His right was His Blessed Mother. Ferdinand saw that he was to be condemned for his wicked life. He called upon the Blessed Virgin, implored her assistance, promised to quit the world, and lead a life of religious penance. His prayer was heard. He awoke, and his cheeks were wet with tears. He remembered the warning, and promised God on oath to enter a religious order.

Next morning Alonso came, and. seeing Ferdinand look sad and troubled, began to banter him, and tried to amuse him by telling him of the gay parties to which they were to go. Ferdinand told him of his dream, and the vow he had made to change his life and enter a convent. Alonso laughed, and said, mockingly: " What! go into a convent? Will you not take me with you? Now, seriously, Ferdinand, you are not such an old woman as to believe in such nonsense? Do you not think that I wish to save my soul too? Indeed I do ; but you see I am in no hurry. Plenty of time when I get old. Don't you know the old saying : ' All's well that ends well' ?" Just at this moment a servant came up-stairs and told Alonso that there were two gentlemen at the door who wished to see him on very urgent business. Alonso told Ferdinand to banish his melancholy fancies and to prepare for the pleasant party they were to attend that evening. He then hurried down-stairs. At the door, he met two young men with whom he had had a quarrel the day before on account of some love-affair. As soon as they saw him, they rushed upon him, stabbed him to the heart, and fled, leaving him weltering in his gore. Ferdinand, hearing the scuffle and the wild, agonizing shriek, rushed down-stairs. To his horror, he found that Alonso was dead. At the sight of this bloody corpse, he was vividly reminded of his dream. He hastened to the nearest church, cast himself at the feet of a priest, related the terrible tragedy, his dream, his vow, made a good confession, and renewed his vow. He was now restored to the grace of God, full of fervor and happiness. He sold his property in order to give the price to the poor. But alas ! after some time his impure passions began to revive, and he did not resist them. Instead of giving his wealth to the poor, he spent it in gambling, drinking, feasting, and debauchery. He cast himself headlong into the whirlpool of impurity. His excesses brought on a sickness. God, in mercy, now gave him another warning : he saw the fathomless abyss of hell open beneath him. He saw in its fiery dungeons thousands of souls horribly tormented by the devils. He saw before him once more his Eternal Judge: In a moment, a swarm of demons rose out of hell to seize his soul and drag him into the fiery gulf.

Again in his agony the unfortunate man called upon Mary, and again he obtained a respite; but something in his heart told him it was to be the last time. He was now changed. He did penance, and was restored to health. But with returning health the accursed habit of sin returned also. His passions grew strong again ; he sought the occasions of sin; he fell, and became worse than ever. Reduced to poverty, he sailed to South America. On arriving at Lima he spent whatever he earned in gratifying his passions, the consequence of which was that he fell sick once more, and went to the city hospital. Again he began to enter into himself. He sent for a holy missionary, who was celebrated for his zeal, and made his confession with a flood of tears. He told the missionary of his vow. The good priest promised to assist him to enter the convent as soon as he should recover, and promised to come and see him again. The young man soon recovered; but no sooner was he well than all his good resolutions were forgotten. In order to avoid the missionary, he left the hospital as soon as possible, and travelled through the country, everywhere giving himself up to the most shameful disorders. Some years afterwards this holy missionary was led by his zeal into one of the wildest and least frequented parts of Peru. There, in a little town surrounded by lofty mountains and pathless forests, he spent some time in instructing the inhabitants and in visiting the hospital. One day, as he was going about from bed to bed, instructing and comforting the sick, he heard a low moaning sound proceeding from a corner of the room. He went thither, and his eyes fell on an object that filled him with horror. There, upon a heap of rotten straw, lay a man, or rather a living, rotting skeleton, for there was nothing left of him but skin and bone. His hollow cheeks, his sunken, lustreless eyes, the intolerable stench that proceeded from his body, which was barely covered with rags, all told too plainly that he was an unhappy victim of that degrading passion which should not be even named amongst Christians. The priest bent over the dying man. The unhappy victim of his own guilty passions slowly opened his languishing eyes, and saw the priest. "Ah, just God!" he cried, in a hollow voice, "are you here? You who alone know all the crimes of my whole life, must you now witness my death?" At these words he began to howl and moan like a wild beast. The priest tried to encourage him, but in vain. "No, no!" he cried, "there is no hope for me. It is too late, too late!" And

36

with a look of wild despair he died, and his guilty soul went forth—no longer in a vision, but in dread reality—to appear before the judgment-seat of God. Ah! how true are the words of the Holy Ghost: "The bones of the impure shall be filled with the vices of his youth, and his impurity shall descend with him to the grave."

What has already been said regards the temporal punishment inflicted in this life on sins against chastity. But what shall the punishment be in the next? You say that God has pity on this sin. But St. Remigius says that few Christian adults are saved, and that the rest are damned for sins of impurity. And Father Segneri says that three-fourths of the reprobate are damned for this vice. The hatred which God bears to sins against purity is great beyond measure. If a lady finds her plate soiled, she is disgusted and cannot eat. Now, with what disgust and indignation must God, who is purity itself, behold the impurities by which his law is violated! He loves purity with an infinite love, and consequently he has an infinite hatred for the sensuality which the lewd, voluptuous man calls a small evil. We may rest assured that, as pride has filled hell with fallen angels, so impurity fills it with the souls of men.

A young student, a model of piety, and who frequented the sacraments, was one morning going to Mass. He met two of his schoolmates, who invited and forced him to breakfast with them in a saloon. He refused; but he was in a manner forced to consent. He took some wine with them; very little at first, but soon liked it, and took more. It began to rise to his head. At this moment his eyes fell on one of the waiting girls. He yielded to the temptation, and was stabbed in the very act of sin. His two companions, terrified, quitted the world, and led lives of rigor and penance in a monastery.

About six years ago, a young man came to one of the

37

Redemptorist Fathers in New York, and said : "Father, be kind enough to hear my confession without delay. I have been so unfortunate as to scandalize a young lady. She died in the very act of sin. A while ago she appeared to me all on fire, and said that she was damned, and that I was the cause of her damnation, of her everlasting torments. I tremble all over, and fear I may die in the same manner. ' The same father was one day called to assist a dying man in a house of ill-fame. But he went in vain. The impure man was dead and judged. He died in the very act of sin. The same punishment was inflicted about two years ago on some young people in one of the New England States. They were found dead in the corn-field in the act of sin.

One day, the Fathers of the Mission of St. Vincent gave a retreat in their house at Florence to a gentleman who had lived in criminal intercourse with a lady, who died before making her peace with God. While this gentleman, in the bitterness of his repentance, was imploring the Divine mercy for the companion of his guilt, she appeared to him, and said : " Do not pray for me, for I am damned"; after which, to convince him of the reality of her apparition, she placed her hand on the table before which he was kneeling in prayer, and the part which she touched received the burnt impress of her hand. This table is still preserved in Naples.*

St. Alphonsus relates that one day a young girl was going to church. On the way she met a young man of her acquaintance. He saluted her, and asked her whither she was going. "I am going to church," she replied. " This is a beautiful day," said the young man. " The sun shines so brightly. You have plenty of time to go to church; come and let us take a short walk." The girl hesitated at first, but she forgot to pray, and at last she consented. They both went out into the fields, and the devil went with

* *Life of St. Alphonsus.*

38

them. The young girl forgot all about Mass. She did not think of the terrible danger to which she exposed herself, and at last when she returned home she was no longer innocent. The young man went away, and she never saw him any more. The girl went home, but she did not tell her parents what had happened, and they suspected nothing. Evening came, and the girl felt unwell. Morning came, and the girl was much worse. A neighboring woman came in, and when she saw the girl she grew pale and whispered to the mother: "For God's sake, send quick for the priest; your daughter is dying." The girl's brother ran in haste for the priest, but he was not at home. He had gone far away on a sick call. The girl's mother went to the window and looked out anxiously, to see if the priest was coming. Suddenly the young girl uttered a fearful scream. The mother ran to the bedside. The daughter was sitting up, her face was deadly pale, her eyes were staring wildly. "My poor child," said the mother, "what is the matter? Why did you scream?" The girl pointed with her finger to a corner of the room and said: "O mother, mother! look, look! Do you not see them?" "No, my child," said the mother, "I can see nothing." "O mother!" screamed the girl in an agony of terror. "See them, those horrible black people. See, they are coming near me." "Do not mind those black people, my darling," said the mother soothingly. "The priest will soon be here, and he will drive them away." And the mother gently laid back the girl's head on the pillow. "Now sleep, my dear child," said she; "the priest will soon be here, and all will be well." She then went once more to the window, and looked out anxiously to see if the priest was coming Again the girl uttered a wild shriek. The mother hastened to her side. The girl was sitting up as before—her eyes glared wildly, looking like two balls of fire. The mother laid her hand gently on her daughter's forehead, and she

39

could feel the blood throbbing against her temple. The girl looked fixedly at a corner of the room. She neither stirred nor spoke, but seemed transfixed with terror. Suddenly she shuddered convulsively, and, turning to her mother, screamed : "O mother, mother, look ! The black people are coming to me. O mother ! they tell me they are devils ; that they are going to carry my soul to hell." And then she began to shriek wildly, and to curse the young man that was the cause of her ruin. She grew black as if she were choking, fell into convulsions, and at last gasped and died. Yes, she died without the priest, died in her sins, and her soul was carried by the devils to hell.

Ah, what a horrible death ! God created this girl for heaven. All that she had to do, to gain heaven, was to avoid bad example and bad company. The moment of temptation came for her ; she did not pray, she did not resist. She broke the commandment of God. She committed a mortal sin, and died without confession or repentance. Had she at least made a good act of contrition, she might yet have been saved ; but no, she died in despair, and the devils carried her soul to hell. The impure may say that the sin of impurity is but a small evil. But at the hour of death they will not say so. Every sin of impurity shall then show itself such as it really is—a monster of hell. Much less will they say so before the judgment-seat of Jesus Christ, who will tell them what His apostle has already told them : "No fornicator or unclean hath inheritance in the kingdom of God." * The man who has lived like a brute cannot sit among the angels. Common-sense, the voice of conscience, Holy Scripture, the Fathers of the Church, all the Saints, even all the devils, tell him so.

All that has been said on this subject has been said, not that any one who has been addicted to the vice of impurity may be driven to despair. but that he may be cured.

* Eph. v. 5.

St. Jude Thaddeus

CHAPTER II.

ST. JOHN the Evangelist was once taken in spirit to the bank of a sea. And behold, as he stood there, a hideous beast came out of the deep sea. It had seven heads and ten horns, and upon its horns were ten diadems, and upon its heads were written names of blasphemy. And the beast was like a leopard, and its feet were as the feet of a bear, and its mouth was as the mouth of a lion. And this monster opened its mouth in blasphemies against God, against His holy name, against His tabernacle, the holy Church, and against the Saints in Heaven. And the dragon of hell gave this beast his own power and great strength, and the beast waged war against the Saints, the children of God.* How great would be our horror were this monster to appear to us ! We should die of fright. And yet, there are many who have been for years carrying in their hearts a far more hideous monster—a monster so horrible that, could we but see it in its true shape, the sight of it would kill us. They have carried this monster in their hearts day and night, waking and sleeping; they have carried it for days and weeks, and for years. And the name of it is drunkenness. The spirit of intemperance every day changes human beings into savage beasts—into the hideous monsters of the Apocalypse with seven heads. These seven heads are the seven deadly sins, which are all found in the drunkard. The drunkard is proud, envious, gluttonous, full of lust, etc. There are, of course, degrees of intemperance, and many

*Apoc. xiii. 1.

42

persons are only at times guilty of this sin. There are many who say that drunkenness is no sin. It is not considered by those outside the Church as a sin, but as a weakness : men speak of it as a misfortune ; physicians class it as a simple mania, to be pitied rather than condemned. Instead of giving to it, as a moral disease, a moral remedy, they encourage it by taking away its enormity. But what says the Word of God ? It tells us that drunkenness is a mortal sin. St. Paul says : " The drunkard shall not possess the kingdom of God."* And why shall not the drunkard possess the kingdom of God ? Because the sin of drunkenness of which he becomes guilty is a grievous sin against nature, against religion, against himself, against the family, and therefore against God, the Author of nature, the Spirit of religion, and the Founder of the family. It goes against nature, because it ruins the body, corrupts the soul, and changes the image of God in man into the likeness of a brute.

It is a singular fact that the devil may tempt a man in a thousand ways. He may get him to violate the law of God in a thousand ways, but he cannot rob him of the divine image that the law of God set upon him in reason, in love and freedom. The demon of pride may assail us, but the proudest man retains these three great faculties in which his manhood consists; for man is the image of God. The image of God is in him ; his intelligence, love, and freedom are the quintessence of his human nature that the devil must respect. Just as of old the Lord said to the demon : "You may strike my servant Job ; you may afflict him ; you may cover him with ulcers; you may destroy his house and his children ; but respect his life ; you must not touch his life." So Almighty God seems to say to the very devils of hell : "You may lead man, by temptations, into whatsoever sins ; but you must respect his manhood ; he must still remain a man." To all except one ! There is one devil

* 1 Cor vi. 9.

alone who is able not only to rob us of that divine grace by which we are children of God, but to rob us of every essential feature of humanity, in taking away from us the intelligence by which we know, the affection by which we love, the freedom by which we act, as human beings, as we are. What demon is this who is the enemy not only of God but of human nature? It is the terrible demon of intemperance. Every other demon that tempts man to sin may exult in the ruin of the soul; he may deride and insult Almighty God for the moment, and riot in his triumph; insult Him as the author of that grace which the soul has lost. The demon of drunkenness alone can say to Almighty God: "Thou alone, O Lord, art the fountain, the source, the Creator of nature and of grace. What vestige of grace is here? I defy you, I defy the world to tell me that here is a vestige even of humanity!" Behold the drunkard. Behold the image of God as he comes forth from the drinking-saloon, where he has pandered to the meanest, vilest, and most degrading of the senses—the sense of taste. He has laid down his soul upon the altar of the poorest devil of them all—the devil of gluttony. Upon that altar he has left his reason, his affections, and his freedom. Behold him now, as he reels forth, senseless and debauched, from that drinking-house! Where is his humanity? Where is the image of God? He is unable to conceive a thought. He is unable to express an idea with his babbling tongue, which pours forth feebly, like a child, some impotent, outrageous blasphemy against Heaven! Where are his affections? He is incapable of love; no generous emotion can pass through him. No high and holy love can move that degraded, surfeited heart. The most that can come to him is the horrible demon of impurity, to shake him with emotions of which, even in that hour, he is incapable! Finally, where is his freedom? Why, he is not able to walk, not able to stand, he is not able to guide himself! If a child came along and pushed him, it would throw him down. He has no freedom left—no will. If, then, the image of the Lord in man be intelligence—in the heart and in the will—I say this man is no man. He is a standing reproach to humanity. He has cast aside his manhood and adopted the habits of a brute. He roars like a lion, he capers like a donkey, he wallows in the mire like a swine. What sort of an animal is he? He is a swine, and worse than a swine ; for what animal is there more filthy and impure than a drunkard, whose very thought, word, and deed reek of impurity! When did a drunken man or a drunken woman commit the most abominable, the most unnatural crimes? When did they degrade themselves below the brute beast? Was it not when their reason was besotted by the accursed vice of drunkenness? Look upon the wretched drunkard as he staggers along the street! The street seems too narrow for him ; his feet are unable to carry their monstrous load. He reels ; he falls ; he wallows in the mire till he is all besmeared with filth. The very dogs come and look at him, smell him, wag their tails, and walk off. They can walk, but he cannot; they find their way home, but he cannot.

And this is the image of God? No ; he is no longer the image of God, because he has lost his intelligence. What says the Holy Ghost? The man blinded, when he has no honor—when he has lost his intelligence—He compares to a senseless beast; like unto it he is no longer the image of God, but only a brute beast. And if such be the sin that the drunkard commits against humanity, what shall be said of the sin that he commits against religion?

The drunkard seldom or never goes to Mass. He never goes to confession. Or, if he does, it is only to lie to the Holy Ghost, for he promises to abstain from drink, and he breaks his promises as soon as he has made them. He is a disgrace to religion, the enemy of the priest, the stumbling-block to nundreds in the way of conversion, a mockery of our holy faith, a wretch who drags his faith in the mire and pollutes the precious blood of Jesus Christ. Go through the streets of any of our large cities, and see a drunkard staggering along and serving as a laughing-stock for the whole neighborhood. Go ask who it is, and to your shame some scoffing infidel will tell you, sneeringly, "Oh! it is only a drunken Catholic!" A drunken Catholic! My God! is it then for this that thou hast come into the world? Sweet Jesus! is this the fruit of thy bitter passion! Is it for this that thou didst bleed and die, to found a pure and holy religion? And is it for this that the priests of God have left father and mother, home and friends, and all that was near and dear to them on earth? Is it for this that they have studied and labored so long—that they have renounced all the pleasures and honors of life? Have they sacrificed all only to become the priests of a people who trample all the dictates of religion and reason under foot, who are the disgrace of their faith, their country, and their God?

When God upbraided the Israelites by the mouth of his prophet, he named all their wicked crimes one by one. ' There is," saith the Lord, " no truth, there is no mercy, there is no knowledge of God among these people. Cursing, lying and murder, and robbery and adultery have overflowed the land ; one bloody deed surpasses the other." And then, as if to sum up all these grievous crimes in one most grievous crime, God says : "These people are become like unto those that contradict the priests." This terrible truth is the last degree of wickedness to which sinners can come ; for he who contradicts the priests of God contradicts God Himself. Our Saviour says to the apostles : " He who despises you despises me." He saddens the Holy Ghost ; and Jesus assures us that he who sins against the Holy Ghost shall not obtain forgiveness, neither in this life nor in the

46

life to come. Now, call together the sinners of every class, seek especially those who by every word and action contradict the priest of God, and foremost among them you will find the drunkard. Yes, the drunkards are those who contradict the priest. The priests tell them that drunkenness is a grievous sin, and they answer that it is only a weakness of nature, more to be pitied than blamed. The priests tell them that they dishonor their faith, that they make themselves a laughing-stock for the enemies of our holy Church, and these unworthy Catholics choose the most solemn festivals, the most sacred days, as the most fitting occasion when to satisfy their accursed passion. The priests denounce the detestable crime of drunkenness. From the altar they protest against it, in the name of God. And these men who have heard them leave the church to go straight to the low haunts of sin and intemperance. They have been implored for the love of God, for the love that they bear to their immortal souls, to give up drunkenness and to lead sober and upright lives. And those very Catholics who have heard such pleadings and prayers in the morning, one blushes to meet in the evening staggering home in their drunken defilement ; and perhaps, ere another day has passed, the priest is sent for to prepare them for an untimely death. What wonder at the fearful vengeance that so often falls upon the drunkard ! Listen to the dread sentence of the Holy Ghost : "The drunkard shall not enter the kingdom of Heaven." Listen to the terrible threat which God has pronounced against them by the mouth of His prophet: " I shall make them drunk till they fall asleep, and sleep that eternal sleep, that knows no waking." *

They shall die as they have lived, they shall die in their sins."

In the year 1872, there was in the poor-house of Crown Point, Lake County, Indiana, a native of Grosslosheim in

* Isaias li. 7.

47

the diocese of Treves, Germany. He had been a rich man, but through his intemperance he was soon reduced to beggary. He came over to this couutry to try and repair his fortune. Here he grew worse and worse ; he fell away from his religion; he renounced his God, and became a bitter enemy of everything sacred. He ridiculed God, he ridiculed religion, he ridiculed the priest, the church, the sacraments, the pious, the saints. Well, death came to him at last. He was missed from the poor-house for some days. No one knew anything of his whereabouts until on the 27th of October, 1872, his bones and clothes were found scattered about—not in the grave-yard, not in the field, not in the streets, but in the pig-sty. Having led the life of a swine, he was eaten up by the swine.

The drunkard sins not only against nature and against religion, but he also sins grievously against himself.

Look at a young man of eighteen or nineteen whose father, mother, or himself have never touched intoxicating drink: he is full of strength and energy, mentally and physically ready for any emergency. Let him begin to drink liquor : he does not become a drunkard suddenly; he sinks by the regular stages ; his liking for drink grows on him slowly but surely, until at last he becomes a regular drunkard. At twenty-seven or twenty-eight he has become a wreck, with tottering feet, trembling hands, glassy eyes : drink has ruined his constitution. The man has been poisoned.

It is known that out of every ten gallons of drink sold nowadays—especially in the low grog-shops—nine gallons are poison. This enters into the system, destroys the coating of the stomach, is absorbed in the blood, and ruins the entire health. The strongest proof of the effects of drink is to be found in the cities, where the terrible epidemics of cholera, typhus, or yellow fever have paid their visits—the first men who fall are the drunkards. Read the statistics of New Orleans, Liverpool, London, and New York, and you will find this to be the fact.

Ah ! yes, the drunkard loses health, loses reputation, loses his friends, loses his wife and family, loses domestic happiness, loses everything. And in addition to this is the slavery that no power on earth, and scarcely—be it said with reverence—any power in Heaven, can seem to be able to assuage. All this is the injury that man inflicts upon himself by this terrible sin.

Finally, consider the evil that the drunkard does to his family. St. Paul says that he "who neglects his family is worse than a heathen, and has already denied his faith." We are bound to love our neighbor. Our neighbor may be a Turk, a Mormon, or an infidel, but we must love him. For instance, we are bound to regret any evil that happens to him, because we are bound to have a certain amount of love for all men. Well, in that charity which binds us to our neighbor there is a greater and a less. A man must love with Christian charity all men. But there are certain individuals that have a special claim on his love that he is bound, for instance, not only to love, but to honor, to worship, to maintain. And who are they ? The father and the mother that bore us ; the wife that gave us her young heart and her young beauty ; the children that Almighty God gave us. These gifts of God—the family, the wife, the children, have the first claim upon us ; and they have the most stringent demand upon that charity concentrated, which, as Christians, we must diffuse to all men. And this is precisely the point wherein the drunkard shows himself more hard-hearted than the wild beast. The woman that in her youth, and modesty, and purity, and beauty put her maiden hand into his before the altar of God, and swore away to him her young heart and her young love ; the woman who had the trust in him to take him for ever and for aye ; the woman who, if you will, had the confiding

49

folly to bind up with him all the dreams that ever she had of happiness, or peace, or joy in this world ; the woman that said to him, " Next to God, and after God, I will let thee into my heart, and love thee and thee alone," and then before the altar of God received the seal of sacramental grace upon that pure love—this is the woman, and her children and his children, towards whom the drunkard cannot fulfil his duties of a husband and a father.

How is it possible for him to do so ?

The drunkard is a husband. Why, his wife is starving and in rags ; he treats her as if she was the vilest slave. The drunkard is a father. Look at his children : they are shivering with cold and crying for bread, while he is spending his last dollar in the bar-room. Whose boy is just arrested for robbery ? He is the drunkard's son. Poor boy ! his unnatural father spent in liquor the little money that might have supported him honestly, and the wretched boy was forced to steal in order to satisfy the cravings of hunger. There is that son, that daughter, taught to drink from their very childhood, brought up in ignorance of their religion, and utterly demoralized by bad example. In early youth, they found the way to the saloon and to the low haunts of sin and shame. They have been taught by their own parents to drink and to curse, and now they curse those very parents, and they raise their guilty hands to strike those who bore them, and thus bring down upon their own heads the terrible curse of God. What slatternly, dirty creature is that with a black eye and a bloated face ? It is the drunken wife. Her husband is, perhaps, far away, working for her support. He sends her the pay which he has earned at the price of hard toil. And little does he dream that these hard-earned wages only help to ruin his family and to make his wife a drunkard.

Rev. Father T. Burke, O.P., relates the following : " I was," says he, " on a mission some years ago in a manufacturing town in England. I was preaching there every evening, and a man came to me one night after a sermon on this very subject of drunkenness. He came in—a fine man: a strapping, healthy, intellectual-looking man. But the eye was almost burned in his head, and was glassy. The forehead was furrowed with premature wrinkles; the hair was steel-gray, though the man was evidently comparatively young. He was dressed shabbily; scarce a shoe to his feet, though it was a wet night. He came into me excitedly after the sermon, but the excitement had something of drink in it. He told me his history. 'I don't know,' he said, 'that there is any hope for me; but still, as I was listening to the sermon, I must speak to you. If I don't speak to some one, this heart will break to-night.' What was his story? Five years before he had amassed in trade twenty thousand pounds, or one hundred thousand dollars. He had married an Irish girl—one of his own race and creed, young, beautiful, and accomplished. He had two sons and a daughter—a woman. He told me for a certain time everything went on well. 'At last,' he said, 'I had the misfortune to begin to drink—neglected my business, and then my business began to neglect me. The woman saw poverty coming, and began to fret, and lost her health. At last, when we were paupers, she sickened and died. I was drunk,' he said, ' the day that she died. I sat by her bedside. I was drunk when she was dying.' 'The sons—what became of them?' 'Well,' he said, 'they were mere children. The eldest of them is no more than eighteen; and they are both transported as robbers to Australia.' 'The girl?' 'Well,' he said, 'I sent the girl to a school where she was well educated. She came home to me when she was sixteen years of age, a beautiful young woman. She was the one consolation I had; but I was drunk all the time.' 'Well, what became of her?' He looked at me. 'Do you ask me about that girl,' he said, 'what became of her?' And as if the man was shot, down he went, with his head on the floor—'God of Heaven! God of Heaven! She is on the streets to-night—a prostitute!' The moment he said that word he ran out. I went after him. 'Oh, no! oh, no!' he said; 'there is no mercy in Heaven for me. I left my child on the streets!' He went away cursing God to meet a drunkard's death. He had sent a broken-hearted mother to the grave; he sent his two sons to perdition; he sent his only daughter to be a living hell. And then he died blaspheming God!"

Again, look at the drunkard. There is stupidity in his face, fire in his brain, and the demon of hatred and anger in his soul. Hear the broken curses, the blasphemies, that flow from his lips. He imagines that every one he meets is his enemy; he fights and quarrels even with his best friends. What sort of an animal is *he?* He is a tiger, and worse than a tiger. Ah! God help his poor wife when he comes home. She once married a kind,-good-natured man; but now that he has turned to drink he has become a tiger. See how he storms about the house, cursing and swearing! He breaks the furniture, he smashes the doors and windows, and alarms the whole neighborhood. Look at his poor children. God help them now! See how they cower and hide themselves away from their own father. Father, indeed! They tremble in deadly fear at the sight of him whom they should love and honor. To them the dear name of "father" is not a name of love. Ah, no! it is a name of hate and terror. They whisper to one another: "Father's drunk again; let us go away." The poor wife tries to calm him, perhaps, with kind words, and what is her return? O shame! O ye men, born of woman, nourished at her breast, hang your heads in shame at such a deed! And you, angels of God, veil your faces lest you witness the heavy blow and the brutal kick. Poor, unhappy wife! God pity her! Was it, then, for this that she sacrificed all that was near and dear to her in the world? Was it for this that she tore herself away from her fond parents, from her loving brothers and sisters, in order to follow him and to love him? Ah! better were it for her, on the day she gave him her hand and heart, had her bridal garment been changed into a shroud. Better were it for her had she lain stiff and cold in her coffin, than to have stood with him as his bride before the altar. On the day he wedded her, he promised before the altar of God, in presence of the holy angels, in presence of the Almighty God, that he would love, honor, and cherish her. And see how he has kept his promise! He has lost his reason; he has degraded his manhood; his once noble nature is now turned into the nature of a wild, ferocious beast. He stamps about the room, swearing by the holy name of God that he will not be dictated to by any living being—man or woman. His glaring eye at last falls upon the prostrate form of his once-loved wife. She is lying on the floor, pale and lifeless. What does he see? What is it that makes him thus start back, horror-stricken? It is blood! Yes, there is blood on the pale face of his lifeless wife; there is blood upon the clothes; there is blood upon the floor; and, before he can collect his scattered thoughts, there is a noise outside: the officers of justice enter. The drunkard—the murderer—is seized and handcuffed; he is hurried to prison; he is tried and found guilty—guilty of murder; and then—his body to the hangman, and his soul —to hell. "The drunkard shall not possess the kingdom of God."

There is nothing more pleasing to God than to be merciful and to spare. Therefore the greatest injury that any man can offer to God is to tie up His hands and to oblige Him to refuse the exercise of His mercy—to tell the Almighty God that He must not; nay, that He cannot, be merciful. There is only one sin and one sinner alone that

53

can do it. That one sin is drunkenness ; that one sinner is
the drunkard : the only man that has the omnipotence of
sin, the infernal power to tie up the hands of God, to oblige
that God to refuse him mercy. No matter what sin a man
commits, if, in the very act of committing it, the Almighty
God strikes him, one moment is enough to make an act of
contrition, to shed one tear of sorrow, and to save the soul.
The murderer, even though expiring, his hands reddened
with the blood of his victim, can send forth one cry for
mercy, and in that cry be saved. The robber, stricken down
in the very midst of his misdeeds, can cry for mercy on his
soul. The impure man, even while he is revelling in his
impurity, if he feel the chilly hand of death laid upon him,
and cry out, "God be merciful to me a sinner!" in that
cry may be saved. The drunkard alone—alone amongst all
sinners—lies there dying in his drunkenness. If all the
priests and all the bishops in the Church of God were there,
they could not give that man pardon or absolution of his
sins, because he is incapable of it—because he is not a man !
Sacraments are for men, let them be ever so sinful—provided that they be men. One might as well absolve the
four-footed beast as lift a priestly hand over the drunkard.
If the Pope of Rome were with him, what could he do for
him while in such a state ? The one sin that puts a man
outside the pale of God's mercy is drunkenness. Long as
that arm of God is, it is not long enough to touch with
a merciful hand the sinner who is in the act of drunkenness.

What greater injury can a man offer to God than to
say to Him : "Lord, you may be just. I don't know that
you don't wish to exercise your justice, but you may
You may be omnipotent ; you may have every attribute.
But there is one that you must not have, and must not exercise in my regard ; I put it out of your power ; and that
is the attribute that you love the most of all—the attribute
54

of mercy"; for the Father in Heaven sees in the drunkard his worst and most terrible enemy.

There lived not many years ago, in an obscure part of a certain city, a poor family. They were poor, for their father was a drunkard. He was a good workman, and had once been a kind father and a good husband. But he became acquainted with bad companions, who led him to the bar-room. From that time forth he became an altered man. He no longer frequented Mass or Confession. His chief place of resort was the public-house. He was often out of employment by reason of his drunkenness, and when he was in want of money he sold the furniture, sold even the very clothes of his wife and children, in order to buy liquor. His poor children were in rags, and they would have starved had not the eldest boy, named Willie, managed to work for them. Many and many a time the poor wife, on her knees, begged her unhappy husband to give up the public-house. But the only answer she got was a bitter curse or a hard blow. Once, when this unhappy man came home drunk as usual, he was in a violent passion, and stabbed his son Willie. The boy recovered, but he had to work very hard in an iron foundry, and within a year after his drunken father had stabbed him he sickened and died. The wretched man still continued to drink, and to ruin himself and his family. God often warned him. God waited and waited, expecting that he would do penance; but the unhappy drunkard heeded neither the voice of man nor the voice of God. His punishment came at last. He lived a drunkard's life, he must die a drunkard's death. In a miserable garret, on the third story, in one of the poorest parts of the city, his poor wife was kneeling and praying for her husband. It was just midnight; and well he needed her prayers. Midnight passed, and he came home drunk again. His head was bleeding, and his face was swollen. He had been fighting with his wicked companions. When

he came into the room and saw that his wife had been waiting for him, he said roughly to her: " Why are you sitting
up and wasting the candle ? I suppose you want to tell the
neighbors about me. If you do not go to bed instantly, I'll
kill you." The poor wife was terrified, but she took cour
age, and said kindly : " You are hurt, my dear. I will get
some vinegar and bathe your face with it." The drunkard
grew furious, and, swearing a terrible oath, said: " If you
don't get out of my sight, I will murder you." The poor
woman was faint and weary from hunger and long watching,
and overcome by weakness and terror, fell back fainting on
the floor. The drunken man stood over her, and his face
glared like the face of a demon. He howled like a wild
beast, and sprang upon his wife, kicked her with his heavy
shoes, and stamped upon her. The neighbors heard the
noise, but they feared to enter, for they knew what sort of
a drunkard he was. They then heard him go down-stairs,
open the door, and walk away. On entering the room they
found the poor woman lying on the floor senseless. Blood
was flowing profusely from her mouth and nostrils. The
priest was sent for in haste, and when he came he found
her dying. She had lived a good life, had gone regularly to
the sacraments ; she had borne patiently, for the love of
Jesus, all the cruel treatment of her husband, and now that
she was dying of that ill-treatment no complaint passed her
lips. She forgave her husband ; she prayed for him with
her dying breath. She received the sacraments, and then
died in peace. The following night a good woman was sitting up, watching by the dead body, and praying for the
departed soul. It was already late in the night—about
eleven o'clock. Suddenly she heard the tramp of footsteps
coming up-stairs. She listened ; the footsteps came on—
on, stopped a little way from the door, then came close to
the door, and stopped again. At last the latch was lifted,
the door was opened a little, and a horrible face appeared

It was the face of the murderer. The woman was so terrified, she could neither speak nor scream. The eyes of the
murderer rolled about and wandered over the room, as if
in search of something. At last he looked in a friendly
manner at the woman. " Woman," cried he hoarsely, " tell
me, where is my wife ? " As he said these words, he strode
into the room, and his heavy footsteps resounded on the
wooden floor. The woman's fright passed away ; she arose,
and, pointing sternly to the dead body of his wife lying on
the bed, said : " There, drunkard, there lies the corpse of
your murdered wife." The drunkard went to the bedside,
and bent for a moment over the dead body. Then in a
wild agony he threw up his hands and cried aloud: " My
God ! she is dead ! she is dead ! What have I done? " He
screamed aloud, and those who heard that scream will not
forget it to their dying day. He clinched his hands, his
lips parted so that all his teeth could be seen, a deadly pale-
ness overspread his face, and he fell heavily on the floor.
The woman screamed for help. The neighbors rushed in ;
they lifted up the wretched man, but he had lost his reason,
and raved like a madman.

The priest was sent for, and when he came he found the
drunkard stretched on a bed from which the dead body of
his wife had been removed. Six strong men were holding
him down, hanging with their whole weight on his limbs.
From time to time he started up and shook off these strong
men as if they had been so many children. The large iron
door-key was put betwixt his teeth, that he might not bite
off his tongue ; and it was horrible to hear the grating
sound of his teeth grinding the iron key. The priest had
to leave, as he could do nothing for the unhappy man. Next
day the priest came again. The drunkard was terribly
changed. His flesh was dried up, and his skin parched by
a burning fever. His arms were pinioned ; for it was dangerous to let him loose. His lips were withered and cover-

ed with a brown crust. There was a dark ring around each
of his eyes, and his eye-balls were red and blood-shot. All
those who saw him trembled at the sight ; for he was in
despair. He had indeed recovered his senses, but it was
only to realize the horror of his unhappy state. The priest
approached the bedside and spoke kindly and gently to the
unhappy man. "My man," he said, "you are now dying
You will soon appear before the judgment-seat of Jesus
Christ. Repent of your sins while you have yet time."
The drunkard glared at the priest with fiery eyes. "What!"
cried he, "repent? Is it to me you talk of repentance?
No, no, no ; there is no repentance for me ! I am damned !
I am damned for ever !". The priest encouraged him and
told him to hope in the mercy of God. "No, no," cried
the unhappy drunkard, " there is no hope, no mercy, for me.
All last night I saw my murdered wife and boy standing by
this bed and threatening me. Sometimes they pointed
with their shadowy fingers to the corner of the room, and
there I saw the damned spirits of hell mocking me. And
then these hellish spirits would crowd around my bed and
bend their horrid faces over me; I was tied, and could not
get away from them. Then they would grin and laugh at me,
and tell me how they would meet me to-night—to-night !—
in hell. No, no, there is no mercy for me ; it is too late, too
late." The good priest tried once more to encourage the unhappy man. He told him how the blessed Jesus had died to
save him. He told him how good and kind a mother Mary is ;
how she obtains pardon even for the most abandoned sinner.
But he spoke to a heart of stone ; the drunkard heeded not
his words. The dying man made no confession. He said that
he could not, that he would not, repent. His blasphemies
were too horrible to be told. It seemed as if the very devil
himself was speaking by his tongue. Sometimes he would
call on those present to hide him from his wife and boy, whose
ghosts, he said, were haunting him. Then he would sing a

few snatches of an immodest song, and talk as if he was again in the midst of his bad companions. Then again he would roar out in a fearful agony, as only a sinner dying in despair can shout. " Oh ! " he would cry wildly, " do you not see the devils coming around my bed ? Ah ! they want to take my soul to hell. See ! see ! the blue flames of hell are rising up around me."

It was just midnight. The hour of retribution had come The drunkard was never more to see the dawn of morning. The window was open, and the heavy bell could be heard through the still night-air ; it struck the hour of twelve. Then the wretched man gave a long and terrible howl, and died. He died and passed from the darkness of midnight to the never-ending darkness of hell. Thus dies the drunkard, and thus will every drunkard die who perseveres in his sin; for the Holy Ghost has said : " The drunkard shall not enter the kingdom of heaven." *

Go now, and drink; call it a friendly glass. Yes, you will gain a friend and lose your God. Go now, and drink ; say that you drink only because of your weak health, because of your hard work. Go and buy your drink ; bring on disease and an untimely death. Ask the doctors, the chemists, and they will tell you how much deadly poison you continually drink in with your liquor. Drink and say that you meant no harm ; you only wished to be a little merry ; that you wished to drown your grief and trouble. Drink now of the intoxicating cup, and hereafter you shall drink of the wine of the wrath of God ; you shall drink of fire and brimstone ; you shall drink of the poison of serpents and the gall of dragons.

Go now, and call your friends around the innocent babe that has just been baptized; go and call your neighbors round the corpse of your dead relative, and drink—yes, drink your fill ; but with your liquor drink in the priest's

* 1 Cor. vi. 10.

tears, drink in the widow's and the orphan's curse, drink in the wrath of your offended God. Go, season and soak your bodies with liquor, and be assured that they will burn all the more fiercely for it in the eternal flames of hell.

And you who sell liquor to drunkards—you whose saloon is the vestibule of hell—you who are in it the devil's recruiting sergeant—you who encourage and fatten upon this accursed crime, stand up now in the presence of your Eternal Judge, and say, if you dare, " Their blood be upon us and upon our children." Go home now, and count all your blood-money you have received for your liquor; count it well, for it is the price of immortal souls, purchased by the blood of Jesus Christ. Count it all ; for it is moistened by the tears of the heart-broken wife and her half-starved children. Hoard it with care ; for every cent of it will surely bring upon you and your family the widow's and the orphan's curse—the curse of the avenging God.

And you who are yet free from this accursed vice, thank God, and beware lest you be led into it by degrees. It is far easier for you to avoid falling into this vice than it is to abandon it after having once contracted it. If you have just begun to contract the sinful habit of drunkenness—if you are already its slave—stop now, and pause where you are. Listen to the voice of your poor wife, whom you have so often ill-treated. Listen to the cries of your poor children, whom you have reduced to beggary and shame. Listen to the voice of the priest of God, who conjures you, for the love of God, for the love of your immortal soul, to give up drinking. Listen to the warning voice of the Holy Ghost, who tells you that the drunkard shall not enter the kingdom of heaven. Listen to the pleading voice of your Saviour, Jesus Christ. Do not ruin that soul for which Jesus Christ has died. Three-and-thirty years did Jesus fast and labor in order to gain your soul. He suffered hunger and thirst; He bore patiently the burning thirst

60

that tormented Him on the cross; He tasted the vinegar
and gall, in order to atone for your intemperance. Will you,
then, ruin that soul for which Jesus suffered so much?
Will you trample on the precious blood of Jesus? Will
you render all his sufferings useless? Ah! save yourself,
while you have yet time, from temporal as well as eternal
misery. You have sinned, and you must do penance. Give
up drinking, and God will accept that as a penance. You
have sinned grievously. You have merited the never-ending torments of hell. Give up drink, then. It may indeed be hard and painful; but remember the miseries of
drunkenness—the never-ending torments of hell are far more
painful. The longer you abstain from drink, the easier
will it be for you to abandon it altogether; and the peace
of conscience you will enjoy, the blessings of God, the
prayers of your family, will give you strength enough
to resist the unhealthy craving for liquor. Pray often ·
approach the Sacraments frequently. Choose a good
confessor, and follow his advice, and God may yet preserve you from the unutterable torments reserved for the
drunkard.

How glorious is the mission of the temperance society!
The members of this society have raised the standard in defiance to this demon that is destroying the whole world.
They have declared that their very names shall be enrolled
as a monument against the vice of drunkenness. They
have thereby asserted the glory of God in His image—man.
The glory of humanity is restored by the angel of sobriety
and temperance; the glory of Christ restored from the dishonor which is put upon Him by the drunkard amongst
all other sinners; the glory of the Christian woman re-
trieved and honored, as every year adds a new, mellowing
grace to the declining beauty which passes away with youth;
the glory of the family, in which the rue Christian son is
the reflection of the virtues of his true and Christian father;

finally, the glory of souls, and the assurance of a holy life and a happy death—all this is involved in the profession which they make to be the apostles and the silent but eloquent propagators of this holy virtue—temperance.

CHAPTER III.

There is one special occasion of sin which must be dwelt upon more at length. It is the reading of bad books. Bad books are, 1, idle, useless books which do no good, but distract the mind from what is good ; 2. Many novels and romances which do not appear to be so bad, but often are bad ; 3. Books which treat professedly of bad subjects ; 4. Bad newspapers, journals, miscellanies, sensational magazines, weeklies, illustrated papers, medical works ; 5. Superstitious books, books of fate, etc. ; 6. Protestant and infidel books and tracts.

There are certain idle, useless books which, though not bad in themselves, are pernicious because they cause the reader to lose the time which he might and ought to spend in occupations more beneficial to his soul. He who has spent much time in reading such books, and then goes to prayer, to Mass, and to Holy Communion, instead of thinking of God and of making acts of love and confidence, will be constantly troubled with distractions ; for the representations of all the vanities he has read will be constantly present to his mind.

The mill grinds the corn which it receives. If the wheat be bad, how can the mill turn out good flour ? How is it possible to think often of God, and offer to Him frequent acts of love, of oblation, of petition, and the like, if the mind is constantly filled with the trash read in idle, useless books ? In a letter to his disciple Eustochium, St. Jerome stated for her instruction that in his solitude at Bethlehem he was attached to, and frequently read, the works of Cicero, and that he felt a certain disgust for pious books because their style was not polished. Almighty God, foreseeing the harm of this profane reading, and that without the aid of holy books the saint would never reach that height of sanctity for which he was destined, administered a remedy very harsh, no doubt, but well calculated to make him alive to his fault. He sent a grievous sickness on him, which soon brought the solitary to the brink of the grave. As he was lying at the point of death, God called him in spirit before His tribunal. The saint, being there, heard the Judge ask him who he was. He answered unhesitatingly, "I am a Christian ; I hold no other faith than Thine, my Lord, my Judge." "Thou liest," said the Judge ; "thou art a Ciceronian, for where thy treasure is, there thy heart is also." He then ordered him to be severely scourged. The servant of God shrieked with pain as he felt the blows, and begged for mercy, repeating in a loud voice, "Have mercy upon me, O Lord ! have mercy upon me." Meanwhile, they who stood round the throne of that angry Judge, falling on their faces before Him, began to plead in behalf of the culprit, implored mercy for him, and promised in his name that his fault should be corrected. Then St. Jerome, who, smarting with pain from the hard strokes he had received, would gladly have promised much greater things, began to promise and to swear, with all the ardor of his soul, that never again would he open profane and worldly works, but that he would read pious, edifying books. As he uttered these words he returned to his senses, to the amazement of the bystanders, who had believed him to be already dead. St. Jerome concludes the narration of this sad history with these words : "Let no one fancy that it was an idle dream, like to those which come to deceive our minds in the dead of night. I call to witness the dread tribunal before which

65

I lay prostrate, that it was no dream, but a true representation of a real occurrence; for when I returned to myself, I found my eyes swimming with tears, and my shoulders livid and bruised with those cruel blows." He tells us, finally, that after this warning he devoted himself to the reading of pious books with the same diligence and zeal that he had before bestowed upon the works of profane writers. It was thus that Almighty God induced him to that study of divine things which was so essential to his own progress in perfection, and destined to do so much good to the whole Christian world.

It is true that in works like those of Cicero we sometimes find useful sentiments; but the same St. Jerome wisely said in a letter to another disciple: "What need have you of seeking for a little gold in the midst of so much dross, when you can read pious books in which you shall find all gold without any dross?"*

As to novels, they are, in general, pictures, and usually very highly wrought pictures, of human passions. Passion is represented as working out its ends successfully, and attaining its objects even by the sacrifice of duty. These books, as a class, present false views of life; and as it is the error of the young to mistake these for realities, they become the dupes of their own ardent and enthusiastic imaginations, which, instead of trying to control, they actually nourish with the poisonous food of phantoms and chimeras.

When the thirst for novel-reading has become insatiable—as with indulgence it is sure to do—they come at last to live in an unreal fairy-land, amidst absurd heroes and heroines of their own creation, thus unfitting themselves for the discharge of the common duties of this every-day world, and for association with every-day mortals. The more strongly works of fiction appeal to the imagination, and

* Epis. ad Furian.

the wider the field they afford for its exercise, the greater in general are their perilous attractions; and it is but too true that they cast, at last, a sort of spell over the mind, so completely fascinating the attention that duty is forgotten and positive obligation laid aside to gratify the desire of unravelling, to its last intricacy, the finely-spun web of some airy creation of fancy. Fictitious feelings are excited, unreal sympathies aroused, unmeaning sensibilities evoked. The mind is weakened; it has lost that laudable thirst after truth which God has imprinted on it; filled with a baneful love of trifles, vanity, and folly, it has no taste for serious reading and profitable occupations; all relish for prayer, for the Word of God, for the reception of the sacraments, is lost; and, at last, conscience and common sense give place to the dominion of unchecked imagination. Such reading, instead of forming the heart, depraves it. It poisons the morals and excites the passions; it changes all the good inclinations a person has received from nature and a virtuous education; it chills by little and little pious desires, and in a short time banishes out of the soul all that was there of solidity and virtue. By such reading, young girls on a sudden lose a habit of reservedness and modesty, take an air of vanity and frivolity, and make show of no other ardor than for those things which the world esteems and which God abominates. They espouse the maxims, spirit, conduct, and language of the passions which are there under various disguises artfully instilled into their minds; and, what is most dangerous, they cloak all this irregularity with the appearances of civility and an easy, complying, gay humor and disposition.

St. Teresa, who fell into this dangerous snare of reading idle books, writes thus of herself: "This fault failed not to cool my good desires, and was the cause of my falling insensibly into other defects. I was so enchanted with the extreme pleasure I took herein that I thought I could not be content if I had not some new romance in my hands. I began to imitate the mode, to take delight in being well dressed, to take great care of my hands, to make use of perfumes, and to affect all the vain trimmings which my condition admitted. Indeed, my intention was not bad, for I would not for the world, in the immoderate passion which I had to be decent, give any one an occasion of offending God; but I now acknowledge how far these things, which for several years appeared to me innocent, are effectually and really criminal."

Criminal and dangerous, therefore, is the disposition of those who fritter away their time in reading such books as fill the mind with a worldly spirit, with a love of vanity, pleasure, idleness, and trifling; which destroy and lay waste all the generous sentiments of virtue in the heart, and sow there the seeds of every vice. Who seeks nourishment from poisons? Our thoughts and reflections are to the mind what food is to the body; for by them the affections of the soul are nourished. The chameleon changes its color as it is affected by pain, anger, or pleasure, or by the color upon which it sits; and we see an insect borrow its lustre and hue from the plant or leaf upon which it feeds. In like manner, what our meditations and affections are, such will our souls become—either holy and spiritual or earthly and carnal.

In addition to their other dangers, many of these books unfortunately teem with maxims subversive of faith in the truths of religion. The current popular literature in our day is penetrated with the spirit of licentiousness, from the pretentious quarterly to the arrogant and flippant daily newspaper, and the weekly and monthly publications are mostly heathen or maudlin. They express and inculcate, on the one hand, stoical, cold, and polished pride of mere intellect, or, on the other, empty and wretched sentimentality. Some employ the skill of the engraver to caricature the institutions and offices of the Christian religion, and others to exhibit the grossest forms of vice and the most distressing scenes of crime and suffering. The illustrated press has become to us what the amphitheatre was to the Romans when men were slain, women were outraged, and Christians given to the lions to please a degenerate populace. " The slime of the serpent is over it all." It instils the deadly poison of irreligion and immorality through every pore of the reader. The fatal miasma floats in the whole literary atmosphere, is drawn in with every literary breath, corrupting the very life-blood of religion in the mind and soul. Thus it frequently happens that the habitual perusal of such books soon banishes faith from the soul, and in its stead introduces infidelity. He who often reads bad books will soon be filled with the spirit of the author who wrote them. The first author of pious books is the Spirit of God ; but the author of bad books is the devil, who artfully conceals from certain persons the poison which such works contain. Written, as they generally are in a most attractive, flowery style, the reader becomes enchanted, as it were, by their perusal, not suspecting the poison that lies hidden under that beautiful style, and which he drinks as he reads on.

But it is objected the book is not so bad. Of what do bad books treat? What religion do they teach ? Many of them teach either deism, atheism, or pantheism? Others ridicule our holy religion and everything that is sacred. What morals do these books teach ? The most lewd. Vice and crime are deified ; monsters of humanity are held out as true heroes. Some of these books speak openly and shamelessly of the most obscene things, whilst others do so secretly, hiding their poison under a flowery style. They are only the more dangerous because their poisonous contents enter the heart unawares.

A person was very sorry to see that a certain bad book was

doing so much harm. He thought he would read it, that he might be better able to speak against it. With this object in view he read the book. The end of it was that instead of helping others he ruined himself.

Some say, " I read bad books on account of the style. I wish to improve my own style. I wish to learn something of the world." This is no sufficient reason for reading such books. The good style of a book does not make its poisonous contents harmless. A fine dress may cover a deformed body, but it cannot take away its deformity. Poisonous serpents and flowers may be very beautiful, but for all that they are not the less poisonous. To say that such books are read purely because of their style is not true, because those who allege this as an excuse sometimes read novels which are written in a bad style. There are plenty of good books, written in excellent style, which are sadly neglected by these lovers of pure English.

To consult those books for a knowledge of the world is another common excuse for their perusal. Well, where shall we find an example of one who became a deeper thinker, a more eloquent speaker, a more expert business man, by reading novels and bad books ? They only teach how to sin, as Satan taught Adam and Eve to eat of the forbidden tree, under the pretence of attaining real knowledge ; and the result was loss of innocence, peace, and Paradise, and the punishment of the human race through all time.

Some profess to skip the bad portions and read only the good. But how are they to know which are the bad portions unless they read them ? The pretext is a false one. He only will leave the bad who hates it. But he who hates the bad things will not read the books at all, unless he be obliged to do so ; and no one is obliged to read them, for there are plenty of good, profitable, and entertaining books which can be read without danger.

There is a class of readers who flatter themselves that bad books may hurt others, but not them ; they make no impression on them. Happy and superior mortals ! Are they gifted with hearts of stone, or of flesh and blood ? Have they no passions ? Why should these books hurt others and not them ? Is it because they are more virtuous than others ? Is it not true that the bad, obscene parts of the story remain more vividly and deeply impressed upon their minds than those which are more or less harmless ? Did not the perusal of these books sometimes cause those imaginations and desires forbidden by Christian modesty ? Did they not sometimes accuse themselves in confession of having read them ? If not, they ought to have done so. Who would like to die with such a book in their hand ? Readers of bad books who say such reading does not affect them should examine themselves and see whether they are not blinded by their passions, or so far gone in crime that, like an addled egg, they cannot become more corrupt than they already are.

See that infamous young man, that corrupter of innocence. What is the first step often of a young reprobate who wishes to corrupt some poor, innocent girl ? He first lends her a bad book. He believes that if she reads that book she is lost. A bad book, as he knows, is an agreeable corrupter ; for it veils vice under a veil of flowers. It is a shameless corrupter. The most licentious would blush, would hesitate to speak the language that their eyes feed on. But a bad book does not blush, feels no shame, no hesitation. Itself unmoved and silent, it places before the heart and imagina tion the most shameful obscenities.

A bad book is a corrupter to whom the reader listens without shame, because it can be read alone and taken up when one pleases.

Go to the hospitals and brothels ; ask that young man who is dying of a shameful disease ; ask that young woman who has lost her honor and her happiness; go to the dark grave of the suicide ; ask them what was the first step in their downward career, and they will answer, the reading of bad books.

Not long ago a young lady from Poughkeepsie, N. Y., who was once a good Catholic, began to read novels. Not long after she wished to imitate what she read, and to become a great lady. So she left her comfortable home, and ran away with another young lady to New York. There she changed her name, became a drunkard and a harlot, and even went so far in her wickedness as to kill a policeman. Here is the story, told in the woman's own words as given in the public press:

Fanny Wright, the woman who killed police officer McChesney, in New York, on the night of November 2, has been removed to the Tombs, and now occupies a cell in the upper tier of the female prison. The clothing stained with blood of her victim which she has worn since her arrest, has been changed. In reply to interrogations she made the following statements respecting her life :

" About ten years ago I was living happily with my parents at Poughkeepsie, in this State. Nothing that I wished for was withheld. I was trained in the Roman Catholic faith, and attended to my religious duties with carefulness and pleasure until I was corrupted by a young girl of the same age, who was my school-fellow. She had been reading novels to such an extent that her head had become fairly upset, and nothing would do her but to travel and see the world. The dull life of a small country place like Poughkeepsie would not suit her tastes and inclinations, and from repeatedly whispering into my ears and persuading me that we would be great ladies, have horses, carriages, diamonds, and servants of our own, I finally reluctantly consented to flee from home, and we started together one beautiful night for the city of New York. [Here the poor woman gave way to tears, and sobbed hysterically.] On our arrival in this city we took up our quarters with Mrs. Adams, at No. 87 Leonard Street, and this was the place where I lost my virtue and commenced to lead a life of bitter, bitter shame. My family ultimately succeeded in finding out my whereabouts and took me home, but I could not listen to the voice of reason. I felt that I had selected my mode of life, and was determined at all hazards to follow it out. I escaped a second time, and went back to Mrs. Adams's, where I was confined of a sweet little girl shortly afterwards. I used to keep myself very clean, and dressed with great care and tastefulness. From Mrs. Adams's I moved to Mrs. Willoughby's, at No. 101 Mercer Street, and lived there until the death of my little girl, three years ago; that had an awful effect upon me ; I could not help taking to drink to drown my sorrow From this period I date the commencement of my real hardships. My father emigrated to California, and I had no one left but a young brother ; he tried to reform me, and also his poor wife ; God bless her ! she used to cry herself sick at my disgrace. Previous to this the young girl who accompanied me from home in the first instance fell out lucky, and got married. Drinking was the only pleasure of my life, and it was not long until it began to have its results ; I was arrested and committed to the Island for six months ; I got down before my time was up, and again took to liquor and street-walking. I used to walk all the time between Greene, Wooster, and Mercer Streets, in the Eighth Ward. I was soon arrested the second time, and sent up again for six months. During the last three years of my life, I have been sent on the Island six times altogether for drunkenness and disorderly conduct. On the night the officer was killed [here she gave way again to tears, and rocked herself around on the bed in a fearful manner], I was walking through the street, going home with message, and picking the kernels out of a hickory-nut

73

with a small knife, when the officer came up to me; I was almost drunk at the time, and much excited; I did not know what I was doing, when on the impulse of the moment I struck him with the knife and killed him." On Tuesday the brother of Fanny, a respectable young man, residing in the neighborhood of Poughkeepsie, called at the prison and had an interview with his sister.

A more affecting scene, says the *Express*, it has seldom been our lot to witness. Although a strong, robust man, he fairly shook with emotion from a keen sense of grief and shame. He remained with her for nearly an hour. She was almost frantic with violent outbursts of grief, and after his departure became insensible.

Another young lady of the State of New York was sent to a convent school, where she received a brilliant education. She spoke seven languages. She wished to enter a convent, but was prevented by her parents. Her parents died, and after their death the young lady took to novel-reading. She soon wished to imitate what she had read; she wished to become a heroine. So she went upon the stage and danced in the " Black Crook." At last she fell one day on Second Avenue, in New York, and broke her leg in six places. She was taken to a hospital, where a good lady gave her a prayer-book. But she flung it away and asked for a novel. She would not listen to the priest encouraging her to make her confession and be reconciled to God. She died impenitent, with a novel in her hand.

Assuredly, if we are bound by every principle of our religion to avoid bad company, we are equally bound to avoid bad books; for of all evil, corrupting company, the worst is a bad book. There can be no doubt that the most pernicious influences at work in the world at this moment come from bad books and bad newspapers. The yellow-covered literature, as it is called, is a pestilence compared with which the yellow fever, and cholera, and small-pox are as nothing, and yet there is no quarantine against it. Never take a book into your hands which you would not be seen reading. Avoid not only notoriously immoral books and papers, but avoid also all those miserable sensational magazines and novels and illustrated papers which are so profusely scattered around on every side. The demand which exists for such garbage speaks badly for the moral sense and intellectual training of those who read them. If you wish to keep your mind pure and your soul in the grace of God, you must make it a firm and steady principle of conduct never to touch them.

Would you be willing to pay a man for poisoning your food? And why should you be fool enough to pay the authors and publishers of bad books and pamphlets, magazines, and the editors of irreligious newspapers for poisoning your soul with their impious principles and their shameful stories and pictures?

Go, then, and burn all bad books in your possession, even if they do not belong to you, even if they are costly. Two boys in New York bought a bad picture with their pocket-money, and burned it. A young man in Augusta, Ga., spent twenty dollars in buying up bad books and papers to burn them all. A modern traveller tells us that when he came to Evora, he there on Sunday morning conversed with a girl in the kitchen of the inn. He examined some of her books which she showed him, and told her that one of them was written by an infidel, whose sole aim was to bring all religion into contempt. She made no reply to this, but, going into another room, returned with her apron full of dry sticks, all of which she piled upon the fire and produced a blaze. She then took that bad book and placed it upon the flaming pile; then, sitting down, she took her rosary out of her pocket, and told her beads until the book was entirely burnt up.*

* *Compitum*, book ii. p. 289.

CHAPTER IV.

ST. ALPHONSUS, in his book *Glories of Mary*, tells of a
poor sinner who, among other crimes, had killed his
father and brother, and was in consequence a fugitive.
One day in Lent, after hearing a sermon on the mercy of
God, he went to confess his sins to the preacher himself.
The confessor, on hearing the enormous crimes which he
had committed, sent him to the altar of the Blessed Virgin,
that she might obtain for him heartfelt sorrow and the pardon of his sins. The sinner obeyed and began to pray.
The sorrow obtained for him by the Mother of God was so
great that he suddenly died from excess of grief. On the
following day, while the priest was recommending the soul
of the deceased sinner to the prayers of the people, a white
dove appeared in the church, and let a card drop at his feet.
The priest took it up, and found the following words
written on it : "The soul of the deceased, on leaving the
body, went straight to heaven. Continue thou to preach
the infinite mercy of God."

The Lord of mercy addresses to every priest the words :
"Continue thou to preach the infinite mercy of God."
There are many sinners who despair of salvation. They give
up all hope of ever recovering the grace of God. Some
say to themselves : "Could I but once more be reconciled
with the Almighty, I would never again commit a mortal
sin. I would lead a far different life." On such sinners
God has mercy, for He sees them ready to profit by His

mercy. He therefore sends them a good priest, a charitable friend, to encourage them to hope in His mercy. He permits them to hear or read a sermon on His goodness to inspire them with the hope of forgiveness. Without delay they cast themselves at the feet of the priest, make a sincere confession of their sins, with the firm purpose of abandoning their sinful lives, and of being, for the time to come, faithful in the service of God.

But there is another class of sinners represented by the prodigal's companions. They, too, are glad to hear the infinite mercy of God extolled. But instead of accepting with gladness the pardon that God so generously offers them, they obstinately neglect His offer. If a young woman who keeps sinful company with a young man is told to leave his company and go to confession, what will be her answer? " O Father ! I cannot give him up now ; I am not yet prepared to go to confession. What would people say if I were to keep company with him no longer ? " If a revengeful woman is told to speak to her enemy, and to make amends for all she has said about her neighbor, what would she say ? " I cannot do it ; I cannot speak to that woman."

If a man is told to restore everything that he has stolen or gained by dishonest means, what answer would he make ? " I cannot do it; I should be reduced to beggary." If a young man who has been for years a slave to sinful habits is asked when he intends to give up his shameful habits and go to confession, " Oh ! " he will say, " I cannot go now, but I will go at some other time. There is time enough to do penance and to be reconciled with Almighty God. I wish to enjoy myself a while. The Lord is merciful. I shall do penance and make a good confession at some other time. at least on my death-bed, and God will forgive me."

Yes, all say : " God is merciful. I shall do penance some other time, and God will forgive me." True. God is merci-

ful. If He were not merciful, who would be living to-day?
And He has even sworn an oath that He will forgive us, no
matter how numerous, no matter how enormous, our sins
may be, provided that we turn to Him with our whole
heart; but without real change of heart, without true,
earnest contrition, God will not, God cannot pardon us—no,
not even for a single venial sin. By putting off our conversion from day to day, we deliberately declare in the
face of Heaven and earth, and renew the declaration every
day, that we will not do penance, even though we have the
power and the time to do so. Of our own free will, therefore, we exclude ourselves from God's mercy and compel God
to condemn us. By putting off our conversion we wilfully
abuse God's mercy and make of it a motive for sinning.
We remain in sin and refuse to do penance because God is
patient and merciful. Does not this partake of the malice
of the devil? Because God is good, we will be wicked ;
because God is merciful, we will remain hardened ; we will
persevere in sin and remain impenitent just because God is
patient and long-suffering. We continue to sin on from day
to day, and from year to year, because God does not punish
us instantly and cast us into hell in the very act of sin.
This course of action is a fearful mistake and misapprehen-
sion of God's kindness to us. If we reject the pardon that
God now so generously offers us, the time will come when
we shall ask for pardon, and it will not be given us. "You
shall seek me," says Jesus Christ, "but you shall not find
me, and you shall die in your sins."

In order to understand aright this fearful truth, we must
remember two other great truths : God numbers, weighs, and
measures all things.   He numbers the stars ; He measures
the drops of rain which He sends upon the fields of the
good and of the bad.   He watches still more carefully over
things of greater importance—over the number of graces
which He has designed for each one of us, that we may

79

work out our salvation. • He also watches over the number
of sins which He is willing to forgive us, over the number
of insults which He is willing to endure from us.   He has
decreed from all eternity how far He will allow each one to
continue in his wicked life.   He has decreed the number of
times that He will grant pardon.   He has resolved on the
measure of sins that He will bear with before utterly for-
saking the sinner.   God waits, perhaps, for a certain sermon, a certain good advice, a certain inspiration ; and if that
inspiration, if that last call, be neglected, then woe to the sinner, for God will call him no more.   The graces which God
had destined for him have been all abused, and shall not be
granted him.   The number of times that God had resolved
to pardon him is exhausted ; the measure of his sins is filled
to overflowing.

God promised Abraham the land of Canaan, but He did
not fulfil His promise until four hundred years had passed
away.   The reason of this was because " the iniquities of
the Amorrhites were not yet filled up." *   That is, the number of their sins was not yet great enough to cause them to be
utterly abandoned by God.   " If they continue to fill up
the measure of their sins," said the Lord, " I will destroy
them all, and give their country to your posterity."

The Lord said to the same patriarch: " The cry of the
abominations of Sodom and Gomorrha has reached my ears ;
the measure of their enormous sins is filled up." †   There
is no more mercy for them ; I abandon them to my justice.

What in each case is this fatal number ?   How great is
this measure ?   The secret is hidden from men.   No one
can know it for certain ; we only know in general that for
some the number of sins is seemingly greater, for others less.
For the angels it seemed very small.   The first sin they
committed caused their eternal ruin.   Millions of souls are
cast into hell for one mortal sin.   The unhappiness of the

* Gen. xv. 16.

† Gen. xviii.

human race comes from one single mortal sin. God made the measure a little greater for the inhabitants of Damascus. He said by the mouth of one of the prophets: "I will pardon three times to the people of Damascus, but if they commit four I will not give them grace to repent."

He gave a still greater number to the children of Israel in Palestine: "They have," said He by Moses, "already tempted me ten times, and have not obeyed my voice ; they shall not see the land I promised with an oath to their fathers." Thus the measure of sin is unequal, the number of offences different. Reprobation begins for some at their first mortal sin ; for others at the tenth ; for others at the hundredth—all depends on the will of God. A master who has two insolent servants may endure the insolence of the one longer than that of the other. Nor is it necessary that the sin which completes this terrible number must be greater than the others ; it is enough that it be the last. The minute preceding the striking of the clock is not longer than other minutes, but it makes the clock strike precisely because it is the last. Sometimes the last sin may even be less enormous than others already committed. To fall into a precipice, it is not necessary that the last step taken be longer than the preceding steps—it may be much shorter ; nevertheless, it is enough to cause the fall.

Now, when the measure of sins is filled up, what happens to the sinner ? One of two things: either he dies immediately, or God still allows him to linger on earth. If he dies immediately, God, without waiting a single moment, casts him into hell. In this way He chastised the rebel angels not leaving them a moment for repentance, as it were, after their sin had been committed. Thus He daily punishes many sinners, carrying them off in the flower of their youth, in the midst of their licentiousness, by a fall, by the stroke of an enemy, or by some other accident.

A young man, a native of Borgo, Taro, a carpenter by

trade, was excessively addicted to drunkenness, and showed himself unwilling in confession to correct this great vice. Father Piamonti consequently dismissed him without granting him absolution. Meanwhile, the young man, instead of entering into himself and repenting, went about boasting that he had been absolved by another priest, and had even received the blessed Eucharist on occasion of the general Communion. For this impiety he was very soon punished in a most exemplary manner ; for the day had not yet passed before the sacrilegious young man received a dangerous wound from the cut of a sword. Every one was persuaded that the misfortune happened to him in punishment of his crime ; but the wretched man fell again into worse disorders than before, and was in a few months visited by divine justice with a more severe chastisement still, being shot dead, without a moment of time wherein to make his reconciliation with God.*

If God does not always punish the sinner immediately when the measure of his sins is full, but allows him still to remain on earth, He withdraws His efficacious graces from him, and delivers him up to a reprobate sense. St. Basil remarks that when a sinner has filled up the measure of his sins his evils become incurable ; he gets outside the circle of God's mercy and into that of His justice, from which he shall never escape

"I shall bear with the citizens of Damascus ; I shall bear with the inhabitants of Tyre ; I shall bear with the children of Ammon until their third and fourth sin, but their fourth sin shall be their last. I shall have mercy on them no longer. I shall punish them, I shall let them die in their sins, and condemn them to eternal torments."

Suppose a man were condemned to quit the country within thirty days at the penalty of losing his life if found within the realm after that time. What would be thought

* *Life of Father Piamonti,* chap. vi.

of him if, instead of making every preparation for his departure, and eagerly seizing the first opportunity to depart, he were to spend his time in drinking and gambling and amusing himself to the last moment ? It would be thought that he had lost his senses. A very similar case is that of one who has committed mortal sin, and who knows that the sentence of eternal death is pronounced against him the moment after the commission of that sin. Death may overtake him at any moment, and if he dies in such a state he will surely be lost for ever. Is it not utter folly to continue so ? Sooner or later that sinful life must be given up if a man has any hope or desire for salvation. This life has been given us to do penance, and yet we have wasted the greater part of it in vain and sinful amusements, in hoarding up perishable riches. We have lost so many good opportunities of abandoning sin, and those opportunities will never return.

But the sinner is apt to think that there is time enough to do penance. "I shall do penance when I am old," he says. But suppose you should die in your youth, because the number of your sins is filled up ? You will do penance next year. But suppose you should die this year, because the measure of your sins is filled up ? What then ? You will go to confession next Easter. But suppose you should never see another Easter, because the number of your sins is filled up before that time ? You will go to confession in a month or two, as soon as you have finished the business that you have on hand. But are you sure that you will live yet another month ? Next week, then, I will give up that bad company, I will restore that money, those ill-gotten goods. But suppose you should die before the end of this week, because the number of your sins is filled up ? To-morrow, then, I will go to confession. To-morrow ? Why not to-day ? Perhaps the morrow will never dawn for you, because the measure of your sins is filled up. I do not think that I will die so soon. That is the very reason why you should fear; for death will come when you least expect it. At last death comes upon you, and you are not prepared. Ah! do not believe the devil; he is your bitter enemy, he is plotting your ruin. Believe rather the priest of God, believe your friends, believe Jesus Christ, who loves you, who has shed every drop of His blood for you. Jesus has your life in His hands; He knows what He says when He tells you that death shall come upon you when you least expect it.

But you say that you will make a good confession and settle everything at the hour of death. Are you sure that at that hour you will be able to make your confession? You may die senseless, you may die without a priest; and what then? Do you not know that it is a terrible thing to fall unprepared into the hands of the living God? Do you not know that, in order to obtain forgiveness of your sins, you must have true contrition? With the grace of God, true contrition is easy of attainment for those who sin through weakness or inattention, because when they are calm and self-possessed they hate sin. Every human heart feels pity for them; much more the all-compassionate heart of God. But as for those who know that they are in mortal sin, and are resolved to remain in it; who continue to sin on with wilful determination; who wilfully reject all the graces that God now offers them; who continue year after year to heap sin upon sin, till the evil becomes a fixed habit, a dire necessity; who knowingly and obstinately continue to sacrifice their reason, their will, their memory, their imagination, their body and soul, their hope of heaven, and God Himself, to sin and to the devil, knowing at the same time that their lives are in the hands of God, that any moment may be their last, that at any moment their guilty souls may be hurried before the judgment-seat of God—for them there is so little hope of true contrition at any future time that

to make them contrite would require a miracle of grace—
a miracle more extraordinary than would be required to
raise a corpse to life.

Many say that they intend to give up sin and do penance
in their old age. But if they give way to all their wicked
passions until they are old, they will not be able to conquer
them in their old age. It may be said that many have enjoyed the world when young, and yet in their old age they
have stopped sinning and have led edifying lives. This
is true. Many have stopped sinning in their old age—that
is, they have stopped committing public and notorious sins.
They have given up the ball-room, the theatre, the house
of infamy. But what does this prove? Does it prove that
they have really given up sin and every affection for sin?
Does it prove that their heart is really changed? Not at
all. If that were the case, then those who are locked up in
the penitentiary would be saints. They do not go to the
ball-room, or to the theatre, or to the house of infamy. But
have they on that account really changed their lives and
given up sin? Open the prison doors and let them free
again, and you will see whether or not they have really
given up sin. This is precisely the case with those old,
hoary-headed sinners who seem to have given up sin. Ex-
teriorly they may have changed, simply because they cannot
help it; but in their hearts, in their desires, they are still
the same. The man who has grown old in sin no longer
goes to the house of infamy, but he goes thither in thought
and desire. Like the snow-crowned volcanoes of South
America, his head is white with snow, but his heart is
burning with the fire of lust.

Who has ever had a racking headache, or toothache, or a
burning fever, and tried to pray or to examine his conscience
while thus suffering? It is almost impossible to pray or
to examine one's conscience while in such a state. But it
is much harder to change the heart, to give up sin, than it

85

is to **pray.** If it is hard to examine the conscience when a person is sick, it is a thousand times harder to do it when dying. And many would put off their conversion to the hour of death. In that last and awful moment, when the memory is confused, who can remember all his sins? In that last moment, when the strength is gone, who will be able to hate sin and love God with all his strength? In that last moment, when speech is lost, who will be able to make a full, sincere confession? How will he who has given scandal be able then to repair all the scandals he has given during his whole life? How will he be able to bring back all the souls that he has led astray and ruined? How will he be able to restore the property and good name of those whom he has injured? Can all this be done in one moment?

Let the sinner look back for a moment on his past life. See how God has called you again and again to give up sin and return to a life of virtue. God spoke to you through the priest; and, lest you should hear the voice of God, you stayed away from the sermon; or if you did go sometimes, it was not to follow the advice of the priest of God, but to criticise and condemn what he had said. God gave you health and abundance, and you used these gifts only to forget and offend the Giver. God brought you to a sick-bed, He reduced you to poverty, and you murmured and blasphemed against Him, saying: "What have I done that God should treat me thus?" God warned you by the terrible examples of those of your acquaintance who had to suffer sickness and poverty on account of sins that were not as grievous as those you had committed. You have seen some even who were hurried out of this life unprepared, and who died in their sins. God sent you these warnings, and yet you did not heed them; you continued to live on as sinful and careless as ever. God called you and warned you through the voice of your conscience. Sometimes He spoke in gentle

tones, sometimes in terrible earnest. Sometimes He en
treated you to give up sin ; sometimes He threatened you with
the fearful chastisement of hell. God spoke to you amid
the hum of business ; He spoke in the silence of midnight,
in solitude, amid the gayest amusements, and in the midst
of your guilty pleasures. Day after day, year after year, He
called you, but you hardened your heart and turned a deaf
ear to all His threats, to all His entreaties. You would say:
" I have no time now to think of such matters ; I will think
of them hereafter when I have more leisure." At another
time you would say: " What great harm have I done ? I
think I am as good as other people." Thus you continually
resisted the Holy Ghost, and stifled the voice of your conscience amid the noisy brawl of the drinking-saloon and the
gambling-table. At last, when conscience ceased to warn
you, you rejoiced, as the worthless son rejoices because his
father is dead and can reproach him no longer. It is thus
God called and warned you ; and though you could have
easily given up sin, you did not. Do you think, then, that
you will be able to give up sin when you are old, when you
are stretched on your death-bed ? No, you will not ; but
you will say : " I have seen several who have led a sinful
life, and yet on their death-beds they sent for a priest, made
a good confession, and died an edifying and a beautiful
death." Yes ! they died such a beautiful death. Ah !
could those souls return to earth, they might tell a different
tale. May God preserve us from such a beautiful death !
They died such an edifying death. Well, it may be, it is not
impossible ; but, in truth, it is very improbable. If such a
sinner was really converted n his death-bed, it was only by
a miracle of God's grace ; and, of course, miracles are possible, but they are not frequent. But should God work
such a miracle for us ? Why not expect that after death God
will raise us to life again, as He has raised many others ?
The careless Catholic, the infidel. the dishonest man, the

drunkard, the member of the secret society, the slave of impurity, men who have despised and mocked the priest during life, are very willing to send for the priest at the hour of death, and to acknowledge that the Sacraments are very useful and even necessary. But are we to understand, by the simple act of sending for a priest at the last moment, that they hate sin and love God with their whole heart? How do such men generally make their confession? One says to the priest : "O Father! I have such a racking headache I cannot remember anything. I include all my sins ; please give me absolution." Another says: "I have nothing particular to confess. I am not a robber or murderer, thank God."

Another loses his speech and dies, without being able to make any confession at all. This is the last confession of such sinners—that confession on which depends their weal or woe for all eternity.

It may be that the dying sinner confesses his sins, kisses the crucifix, and receives the Sacraments ; but is his contrition sincere and supernatural ? Does he weep for having offended God, for having lost Heaven and deserved hell ? Not at all. He is sorry merely because he must die so soon, because he is about to receive the just punishment of his crimes. This is the case with the careless Christian on his death-bed. Could he by the special favor of God recover from his sickness, he becomes just as careless as ever ; he goes back to his old habits, he despises the priest, and laughs at his own fears for having been so easily frightened. A doctor was attending a young woman who had led a very unchristian life. Before her death she sent for the priest, made her confession, and received the last Sacraments with every sign of true contrition. The doctor was naturally astonished at such a sudden change in his patient, and after the priest had departed said to her : "Are you, then, really in earnest ? If you were to recover, would you really give up sin and lead a virtuous life ? " The woman laughed and said, " You must think that I am very silly ; I have not even the remotest idea of such a thing." " Why, then," asked the doctor, "did you go to confession and receive the Sacraments ? " " Oh! you see," was her answer, " one should not be singular. It is the custom when people are dying to send for the priest. As soon as I get well I will try to make up for all the time I have lost here." Such sacrilegious hypocrisy may fill us with horror; but there are hundreds and thousands of persons that lead a bad life who receive the last Sacraments with no better dispositions than this woman.

There is a man who has been a careless Catholic for years and years. He never went to confession, never went to his Easter duty. He was a member of a secret society. He looked with pity and contempt upon those who went regularly to confession. Religion, he thought, was good enough for women. He often said, especially when he was in the company of Protestants and infidels, that one religion was as good as another ; that it mattered little what a man believed, provided he was honest. He turned a deaf ear to the words of the priest. He was very much inclined to think, too, that religion was, after all, an invention of the priests ; that he could get on much better without it. This man falls sick at last ; he is at the point of death. His friends and relatives send for the priest. The dying man makes a hurried confession ; he presses the crucifix to his lips ; he is anointed ; and he dies, and his soul goes where ? To heaven ? Can we believe that our Lord will say to such a man : " Come, good and faithful servant ; you have believed everything that I taught through my holy Church ; you have always loved and practised your holy religion—enter into the kingdom of heaven " ?

If that man gets to heaven so easily, then those Catholics who practise their religion, who fast, pray, give alms, con fess faithfully, would be the greatest fools ; all those converts who have made so many sacrifices in becoming Catholics would be madmen. If it be so easy to get to heaven, then the holy martyrs who shed their blood for the faith would be fools. Those generations of Irish Catholics who suffered poverty, and hunger, and exile, and death, rather than deny their holy faith, were fools and madmen. If it be so easy to get to heaven, Catholics may as well stay away from Mass, from confession, enter as many secret societies as they please, speak against the priests, turn Protestants, or Jews, or infidels. All they have to do is on their death-bed to send for the priest, kiss the crucifix, strike their breasts, and after death they will go straight to heaven. Can we believe this?

Another man has defrauded his neighbor or the Government; grown rich by dishonest speculation or by selling liquor to drunkards. He has stolen the clothes from the drunkard's wife and the food from the mouths of the starving children. At last he falls sick. His relatives send for the priest. The dying man makes a hurried confession; he is anointed; he dies. And his soul goes where? To heaven? What! is it possible to think that he can restore in a few moments all that he has defrauded and stolen during his whole life? Can we think that God will say to him: "Come, good and faithful servant; you have always been honest, you have been faithful even in little things—come, I will place you over great things; enter into the joy of your Lord"?

Another man has spent years grovelling in the very sink of impurity. He has defiled soul and body by the most shameful sins. And now this monster is dying. The priest is sent for. The cries of ruined souls are ringing in the ears of the dying wretch. The curse of Jesus Christ is on him: "Woe to him that scandalizes one of these little ones. It were better that a millstone were tied around his neck, and that he were drowned like a dog in the depths of the sea." The priest may bless the dying man; he may sprinkle holy-water around him; he may pronounce the words of absolution; but the dying sinner hears around him the mocking laughter of demons. The priest of God anoints him, presses the crucifix to his lips, prays for him, weeps for him. He is dead. He is judged. His soul is in eternity. Is it saved? Is it in heaven? What! will God say to that polluted soul: "Come, good and faithful servant; you have preserved your baptismal innocence; you have kept soul and body pure and undefiled—come, enter then into the joy of the blessed"?

Let us not deceive ourselves any longer. To make a good confession, to be truly sorry for all our sins, to detest them sincerely, to be firmly resolved never to commit them again, to undergo cheerfully all the punishments due to them— all these are pure, free gifts of God. Now, the Lord has called us so many times to repentance, and as many times have we refused to hearken to his calls. He has sent us so many warnings, and we have as often turned a deaf ear to them all. We have, then, good reason to believe that the measure of our sins is nearly filled up. We have just as good reason to believe that the number of graces needed to work out our salvation may be soon exhausted. If we do not profit by the few that may be left, we shall infallibly be lost. The grace of God has its moments. Its light shines and disappears. The Lord approaches and withdraws. He speaks and is silent. Master of His gifts, He attaches them to such conditions as He chooses. Such is the ordinary cause of His providence. Choice graces are, generally speaking, a recompense for faithful correspondence with preceding graces. If we do not correspond with them, we become unworthy of greater favors. To what a degree of sanctity and happiness may we not be raised by a moment of grace well used! But a moment of grace neglected may also cast us to the bottom of the abyss.

Abraham will be blessed for ever for having been faithful to the command of God to sacrifice his son Isaac; and Saul will be a reprobate for ever for not having obeyed, on one occasion, the voice of the Lord.

What would have become of David, of St. Peter, of St. Mary Magdalen, had they not profited by the favorable opportunity, by the moment of grace, which was for them the moment of salvation? Happy would Jerusalem have been had it still made a good use of the last day of grace which the Lord gave it. It was her day: *In hac die tua*—" In this thy day." * But this indocile people shut their eyes in order not to see at all. They still resisted the impulses of grace, the tender invitations of God's mercy. They let the decisive moment pass away. Hence their blindness and their misfortune for all eternity. " Jerusalem, Jerusalem, who killest the prophets and stonest them that are sent to thee for thy salvation, how often have I wished, by my preaching, by my example, by my miracles, by my promises, by my threats, and by all possible means, to gather thy children, to draw them to myself with tenderness and affection, as the hen doth gather her chickens under her wings when she sees them pursued by a bird of prey, and thou wouldst not. To punish thine infidelity, I abandon thee to the fury of thine enemies. Thy habitation shall be made desolate." † Jesus says, " How often"—behold the number of graces given for thy salvation; "Thou wouldst not"— behold the refusal of man; "Thou shalt be deserted"— behold his reprobation and chastisement.

Let us turn our eyes for a moment to the heights of Calvary. We see there three crosses erected. On the middle cross hangs Jesus Christ, the Redeemer of the world, while two thieves are hanging beside him, one on the right hand, and one on the left. Jesus created these two men. He created them in love. He created them for heaven. He

* Luke xix. 42.　　　92　　　† Matt. xxiii. 37.

died for both. He shed His heart's blood to redeem the one as well as the other. He offered grace and forgiveness for the one as well as to the other. Both men were great criminals. They were, as Holy Writ assures us, highway robbers and murderers.* Both were seized and cast into prison; both were condemned to the death of the cross; both were actually dying in the very presence and by the side of Jesus Christ. Both are dying; and both of them are still blaspheming, even with their dying breath. They are blaspheming the God who created them; they are blaspheming the Redeemer who is bleeding and dying for them ; they are blaspheming the eternal Judge who in a few moments will decide their fate for all eternity.

These two sinners are dying by the very side of that loving Redeemer who prays aloud even for his murderers. They are both witnesses of the wonderful patience, the God-like meekness, of Jesus in the midst of His sufferings, as well as of the extraordinary miracles that accompany His death and attest His divinity. They see the sun grow dark at midday ; they see the earth shaken and the rocks rent asunder ; they see the graves burst open and the dead come forth to bear witness to the divinity of Him who hangs between them on the cross.

And now for each of these sinners the decisive moment has come—that awful moment on which depends their eternal salvation or eternal damnation. Up to this moment the lives of both have been much alike. They have walked the same path of sin, they have received the same graces, they have shared the same punishment ; and now at the last moment comes a change. One of the criminals opens his heart to the grace of God, while the other wilfully rejects it. One corresponds with the last impulse of grace ; the other remains cold, hardened, and impenitent. Henceforth their lot is entirely different. " One is taken and the other is left."

* Luke xxiii. 33.

God ordered Josue to command the priests to go seven times around Jericho, sounding trumpets of jubilee—that is, of penance and pardon—and bearing the Ark of the Covenant, wherein were kept the tables of the law, some manna, and the rod of Moses; assuring him that at the seventh time the walls would fall of themselves; that he should enter the city with his army, put all the inhabitants to death, and burn it entirely, pronouncing a malediction against him who would attempt to rebuild it.

God here shows us how He goes around our hearts a certain number of times, how He causes to resound in our ears the trumpets of jubilee—that is to say, interior and exterior graces. He uses the manna of consolation to attract us, and the rod of His paternal chastisement to correct us; but after these tours of mercy, if the sinner is not converted, the last tour finished—that is, the last grace given—he is abandoned to justice and condemned to eternal fire.

St. Bonaventure relates that a rich man of a very disorderly life, named Gedeon, was attacked with a most dangerous illness, of which it was expected he would die. He had recourse to St. Francis, who by his prayers cured him, at the same time warning him to change his life, lest something worse should befall him. This wholesome warning, his health miraculously restored, the sickness, were three graces from God to him for his salvation; but the unhappy man abused them. No sooner had he recovered his strength than he relapsed into his former disorders. But by a just chastisement of God it happened that while asleep in his bed the roof of his house suddenly fell in, and he awoke in the eternal flames of hell.

We may rest assured that if we do not now correspond to the grace of God, if we do not follow the good thoughts, the holy inspirations, the remorse of conscience, the invitation of the priest, the entreaty of our friends, but continue to despise all these graces, God will at last withdraw His effi cacious graces from us, and leave us only sufficient graces by means of which we may possibly work out our salvation, but will not do so. Then follows a reprobate sense. The understanding becomes darkened, the will grows weak and stubborn to good, the heart is hardened. We no longer see our danger, we care not for God's threats, we are as insensible as a corpse. When the impious man falls into the depths of iniquity, he despises, says Holy Scripture,* he laughs at everything sacred, at the most serious warnings and menaces of God, at eternal torments. All seems to him imposture ; he grows bolder as he goes on, and even rejoices in the evil he commits. Melted wax resumes its hardness when it is removed from the fire, because it is no longer exposed to the heat of the fire, which caused it to melt. In like manner, by putting off our conversion we place our understanding and will in so dangerous a state that they are no longer sensible to the impressions of grace, which they formerly received so easily. By opposing the movements of grace we become too weak to be able to obey those movements when they come, even though they should of themselves be strong enough to touch the heart.

What a fearful thing it is to persist in resisting the grace of God ! Those who do so incur the further danger of rejecting the decisive grace, throwing away the final moment on which depends their eternal well-being. Would that men could be brought to reflect seriously on this great truth ! But it is what they least think of, though they stand every moment on the threshold of eternity. Certainly, he who, with closed eyes, should run and dance on the brink of a frightful precipice, would deservedly pass for a fool, because he invites a horrible death. Yet the greater part of men are no wiser; for they pay so little or no attention at all to what will be their eternal fate. They fear to lose their wealth, their friends, their honor ; they are afraid of the

* Prov. xvii. 3.

passing sorrows of this life; but they never tremble to contemplate the frightful torments of the next. Dives began to think of heaven only when he was irrevocably plunged into hell by his crimes. Need we wonder at what we read in the Gospel: "Wide is the gate and broad the way that leadeth to perdition; and many there are that enter it. How narrow is the gate and strait the way that leadeth to life, and how few there are that find it." * These terrible words were spoken by our Lord Jesus Christ Himself. They are, therefore, infallibly true, and confirm what our Lord said on another occasion: "Many are called, but few are chosen." God has indeed the greatest desire to save all men; yet all are not saved. He made heaven for all, yet all will not enter into it.

One day St. John Chrysostom preached in the city of Constantinople. "How many in this city," said he to his hearers, "do you think will be saved? How shall I answer the dreadful question, or ought I to answer it at all? Among the thousands of men and women who throng this city, perhaps hardly a hundred will be saved. And would to God that I were certain of the salvation of so many!"

We read that when St. Bernard died, a holy anchorite, who died at the same time, appeared to the Bishop of Langres, and told him that thirty thousand men had died at the same moment, and that only St. Bernard and himself, who had gone straight to heaven, and three souls who had been sent to purgatory, were saved out of that vast number.

A man who had died from the violence of his contrition was afterwards restored to life by the prayers of a holy religious. He said that sixty thousand souls from all parts of the earth were presented with him before the divine tribunal to be judged, and that only three of them were sent to purgatory, and all the rest were condemned to eternal torments.

A doctor of the University of Paris appeared, after his

* Matt. vii. 13.

96

death, to the bishop of that city, and told him that he was damned. The bishop asked him if there was any knowledge in hell. The unhappy wretch answered that he only knew three things: 1. That he was eternally damned. 2. That his sentence was irrevocable. 3. That he was eternally condemned for the pleasures of the world and the body. Then he asked the bishop "if there were still men in the world." "Why?" asked the bishop. "Because," said he, "during these days so many souls have fallen into hell that I thought there could not be many more remaining."

Alas! the number of those who follow their passions and unruly appetites, who constantly transgress the commandments of God, is considerably greater than the number of those who comply with their religious duties. "How can you be astonished if I say that few will be saved," asks St. John Chrysostom, "when you see so many wicked in youth, and so many others negligent and lukewarm in old age? What vanity among women, what avarice among merchants, what pride among the learned, what injustice among the judges, what corruption in all!"

God does not wish to save man by force. He does not wish to destroy the nature of things, but to preserve it. He allows the nature of each being to act in the way that being wills. He made man a free being; He endowed him with a twofold liberty—with the liberty to labor for his salvation or for his damnation. He therefore does not compel men to accept salvation against their will. Where is the man who drags another, in spite of himself, to his banquet? This would be offering an outrage instead of conferring an honor. People are punished against their will, but they are not rewarded in like manner. Reward is given to merit, and we cannot acquire merit unless we are willing to take pains to acquire it.

All who are sent to hell are sent there against their will;

97

out heaven is open only to those who wish to enter there, and who strive earnestly for their salvation.

As long, then, as we put off our confession and live in sin, we shall continue to be the enemies of God; and if we die in that state, we shall infallibly be lost. The moment, however, that we give up sin and make a good confession, our sins are washed away, and we become children of God. Why, then, do we wait? Why do we hesitate? Why do we put off our confession till to-morrow, when we can make it so easily to-day? God offers us pardon and grace now; we have time and ability to make a good confession. To-morrow, perhaps, it will be no longer in our power to do so; we may be in eternity. Now is the acceptable time, now is the time of salvation. If we will do penance now, God will accept it. Our dear Saviour now knocks at the doors of our hearts; He calls us, He entreats us to return to His friend. ship. He promises to forgive us everything if we come to Him with a contrite heart. We can still pray, we can examine our conscience, we can confess our sins; and the priest is awaiting us in the confessional with a compassionate heart. Let us listen to the voice of our friends and relatives, who love us; to the voice of the priest, who wishes us well; to the voice of our conscience, which is the voice of God. Let us not resist that voice any longer, otherwise it will become silent, and then woe to us! what will become of us? We have now every reason to hope for forgiveness; if we delay longer, our hope will be turned into despair. Now the grace of God enlightens our mind and touches our heart. Let us not resist that grace, which has been purchased for us by the tears and by the blood of Jesus Christ. If we hesitate longer, this grace will pass away, never to return.

He who does penance only in his old age or on a death-bed, when he can sin no longer, when the world rejects and despises him -such a one has every reason to fear that his penance is insincere and worthless, because his penance is not free ; it is only prompted by natural, slavish fear. On the contrary, if we do penance while we have the power to commit sin, while the world, with its sinful pleasures, invites us, we show clearly that we are in earnest ; we have every reason to hope for pardon ; and the thought of so noble a deed will be our greatest consolation at the dread hour of death. Is it so very agreeable, so very honorable, to be a slave of the devil, to be bound by the chains of the most shameful sins, the most degrading passions ? Is it prudent, is it reasonable, to live thus longer in mortal sin, when we know that every moment may be our last, and that, if we die as we stand, we shall infallibly be lost ? Let us show that we are not cowards; that we can trample human respect under foot ; that we dare practise openly the dictates of our conscience ; that we are humble and honest enough to go to confession, no matter what others may think or say about us. And even if we cannot finish our confession at once, it is well to make at least a beginning. We shall find that it is not so difficult a thing as we imagine. Arise ! then ; delay no longer. " Now is the acceptable time, now is the day of salvation."

The Lord is loving unto man, and swift to pardon, but slow to punish. Let no man therefore despair of his own salvation.

St. Cyril of Jerusalem: *Catechetical Discourses,* 2, 19. (4th cent.)

S. PETRVS ET S. PAVLVS

Sin, Remission of

For first of all the Lord gave that power
[i.e. to remit sins] to Peter, upon whom
He built His Church, and whence He
appointed and showed the source of
unity—the power, namely, that whatsoever He loosed on earth should be loosed
in heaven.

St. Cyprian: *Letters,* 72, 7. (3rd cent.)

CHAPTER V.

WHILE a pious missionary was one day travelling in one of the wildest regions of North America, he stopped at the principal villages, and often found in them savages whom grace brought to him from a considerable distance. He instructed them, baptized those whom he thought well disposed, and then went on his way to other places. On one occasion an Indian full of fervor presented himself. As soon as he was well instructed in our holy religion, the missionary baptized him and gave him Holy Communion.

A year after the missionary returned to the place where this Indian convert dwelt. As soon as the latter was aware of the missionary's arrival, he ran to throw himself at his feet. He knew not how to express his joy in seeing again him who had begotten him to Jesus Christ. He entreated the father to grant him once more the happiness he had made him enjoy the year before. "Of what happiness do you speak?" asks the missionary. "Ah! my father, do you not know? The happiness of receiving the Body of my God?" "Most willingly, my child; but first you must go to confession. Have you examined your conscience well?" "Father, I examined it every day, as you charged me to do last year." "In that case, kneel down, and declare to me the faults into which you may have fallen since your baptism." "What faults, father?" "Why, the grave faults you may have wilfully committed against the commandments of God and the Church." "Grave faults?" answered the Indian, all amazed. "Can any one offend

101

God after they are baptized, and especially after having received Communion ? Is there anywhere a Christian capable of such ingratitude ? " Saying these words, he burst into tears, and the missionary too could not help weeping as he blessed God for having prepared for Himself, even in the remotest places, worshippers who may indeed be called worshippers in spirit and in truth.*

After having become by baptism children of God and tabernacles of the Holy Ghost, we should cease to offend Almighty God. After the pardon granted in baptism, it would be but justice to sin no more. It would be a pleasing sight to see the child grow up to manhood and old age, and bear unsullied with him to heaven the white robe of his first innocence. Yet how small is the number of those happy Christians who never commit a mortal sin ! Such is the weakness, such is the wretchedness, of human nature ! Alas ! what a misfortune for a soul to lose her baptismal innocence. The purity of that first innocence is so spotless that all other purity seems tarnished, as it were, in comparison with it.

Were God to punish us immediately after we have fallen into sin, what would become of us ? But the infinite goodness and mercy of God have prepared a road for His prodigal child, for every poor sinner to return to His friendship. The Sacrament of Penance is this blessed road on which God stretches out His merciful hand to the repentant prodigal as a sign of pardon and that He will change the soiled robe for a new garment of innocence.

But this duty of confessing our sins seems a hard one to fulfil, and for this reason unbelievers, heretics, and bad Catholics object to confession. It is a doctrine of the Holy Catholic Church that we must either confess our sins or burn in hell. There is no other alternative. Listen to the words of the Holy Church : "If any one says that it is not

* Debussi, *Nouv. Mois de Marie,* 135.

necessary to confess all and every mortal sin, even the most secret sins—all that one can call to mind after a diligent examen—let the same be anathema; let him be accursed." This alone is sufficient proof for every good Catholic; for the voice of the Church is the voice of God.

The practice of confession is as old as the world itself. The first person to hear confession was Almighty God Himself. The first sin that was ever committed on earth had to be confessed before it was pardoned, and God pardoned no one without confession. Our first parents, Adam and Eve, ate of the forbidden fruit, and thereby committed a mortal sin. Almighty God called Adam to account; Adam confessed his crime. "Yes," he said, "I did indeed eat of the fruit, but it was my wife that gave it to me." Eve also confessed her crime, and put the blame on the serpent: "I did eat the fruit," said she, "but it was the serpent that deceived me." Our first parents confessed their sin, they repented of it, and God pardoned them, and even promised them a Redeemer.

Cain also committed a mortal sin: he murdered his innocent brother. But Cain refused to confess his crime, and God granted him no pardon. God called Cain to account, and asked him: "Where is thy brother Abel?" And Cain answered impudently: "I know not; have I then to keep watch over my brother?" And God cursed Cain, and set a mark upon his brow, that he might serve as a warning to all men.

God not only heard confession Himself, but he gave a positive command requiring confession of sins. It would be tedious to cite all the passages of the Old Testament wherein this command is clearly specified. One alone is sufficient: "Whosoever shall commit a sin and carelessly transgress the commandments of God, the same shall confess his sin and restore." * Moreover, the Jews were commanded to

* Numbers v. 6. 7; Lev. xxvi. 40; Prov. xxviii. 13.

bring an offering according to the nature of their sins; for each sin had its own specified offering. It is then clear that they had to confess their sins to the priests, that he might be able to offer the suitable sacrifice.

Not only the priests of the Old Law, but the prophets also, heard confession. King David committed a grievous crime. In order to gratify a sinful passion he put an innocent man to death, and then took away that man's wife. God sent his prophet to the king to upbraid him for his wickedness, and the prophet related to the king the following touching parable : " There lived," said he, " in a certain city two men ; the one was rich, the other was poor. The rich man had a great many sheep and oxen, but the poor man had nothing at all but a little lamb he had bought at a great price. He nourished it with great care. It grew up in his house with his children ; it ate of his bread, it drank of his cup, it slept in his bosom, and he loved it as a daughter. Now, a stranger came one day to the house of the rich man, and there was a great feast. But the rich man spared his own sheep and oxen, and took the poor man's lamb ; he killed it, and served it up to the stranger." King David, on hearing this, was exceedingly angry, and he cried out : " I swear by the living God that the man that has done this deed shall die, and shall restore the lamb fourfold ; for he has had no mercy." Then the prophet, looking sternly at the king, cried out : " Thou art the man ; it is thou who hast done this deed. Listen now to the word of the Lord thy God : I have anointed thee king, I have delivered thee from the hands of thine enemies, I have given thee thy master's house and possession ; and if these were little, I would have bestowed upon thee far greater gifts. Why, then, hast thou despised me, thy Lord and God, and murdered an innocent man, and taken away his wife ? And now, because thou hast done this deed, the sword shall destroy thy children ; I will raise up evil against thee out of thine own house. Thou hast dishonored me in secret; but I will dishonor thee and thy household in the sight of the sun, before the eyes of the whole world; and this thy child, the fruit of thy sin, shall die." On hearing this, King David was terrified and conscience-stricken. He humbled himself before God and His prophet, and confessed his sin, and the prophet, seeing the king's repentance, pardoned him in the name of God. "Now God has taken away thy sin," said the prophet, "thou shalt not die."

The example of the great St. John the Baptist, the last prophet of the Old Testament and the first of the New Law, shows us more clearly how customary it was among the Jews to confess their sins. The Evangelist says that the "people came to St. John from all directions, and he baptized them, and they confessed their sins."* Even at the present day the practice of confession still exists among the Jews in many parts of the world.

Confession, then, was in use in the Old Law, but it was and is also in the New Law. Men sinned in the Old Law; men sin also in the New. Our Blessed Saviour Jesus Christ tells us expressly that He came not to destroy the law, but to perfect it.† When our divine Saviour came on earth, confession of sin was already in use not only among the Jews, but also among the heathens. That confession was in use among the heathens is a fact proved by such abundant and such incontestable evidence, that to deny it is to betray a very gross ignorance of history. It is an undeniable fact that confession was in practice among the pagans of Greece and Rome. No one, not even the emperor himself, could be initiated into their mysteries without first confessing his sins to one of their priests. In Egypt, in Judea, in China, in Peru, the same practice of confession was strictly observed. Even at the present day, confession is practised among many heathen nations. In China, in

* Matt. iii. 6.   † Matt. v. 17.

Thibet, in Siam, in Judea, in Persia, the heathens still confess their sins to their heathen priests, just as they did two thousand years ago. Not only the Jews, then, but the heathens also, confessed their sins.

Our divine Saviour perfected this universal custom, this express law, of confession by raising it to the dignity of a sacrament, and thereby rendered it even still more binding. It is this circumstance, and this alone, that can account for the remarkable fact that the sacrament of confession never met with any opposition either on the part of the Jews or on the part of the heathens. It appeared quite natural to them, for they had been accustomed to it even from the beginning of the world.

God Himself heard confession in the Old Law; God Himself also, the Son of God, our Blessed Saviour Jesus Christ, heard confession in the New Law.

It was about noon, one warm summer's day, that our divine Saviour came with his disciples to the well of Jacob, not far from the town of Sichar, in Samaria. Hungry, and thirsty, and footsore from his long journeys in search of erring souls, He sat down beside the well, whilst his disciples went into the city to buy food. And Jesus sat there all alone beside the well, his head resting on his hand. There was an expression of longing desire on His divine countenance, for He expected some one. And a certain woman came out of the city to draw water. Jesus said to her: "Give me a drink." The woman was surprised and touched by the great condescension, for the Jews despised and hated the Samaritans. "How is it," said she, "that you who are a Jew ask a drink of me who am a Samaritan? for the Jews do never associate with us Samaritans." "Woman," answered Jesus, "if you knew the gift that I have to bestow, if you knew who I am that speak to you, you would ask a drink of me, and I would give you living water." "Good sir," said the woman, "you have no vessel here and the well is deep, how then can you give me this living water ?" Jesus answered : " Whoever drinks of this water shall thirst again, but he that drinks of the water I have to give, shall not thirst for ever. Yea, it shall become in him a fountain of living water, springing up into eternal life." Now came the moment for which Jesus had sighed and waited with such anxiety. This poor woman felt in her heart a great desire to drink of this living water. " Good sir," said she, " give me this water, that I may not thirst any more, and then I need not come here to this well." This is the course which the Saviour always pursues in winning souls. He first awakens in the heart of the sinner a great desire to receive His graces, and then He purifies his soul, and shows him his own misery, and thus prepares him for his graces.

The Samaritan woman begged Jesus to give her this living water, and Jesus immediately said to her : "Go and call your husband." A strange command. Where, one might ask, is the connection here ? The woman asks for the living water, and Jesus tells her to go and call her husband. Now begins this poor woman's confession. " Call your husband," said Jesus. The woman cast down her eyes and answered quietly : " Good sir, I have no husband." " You have said the truth," answered Jesus ; " you have no husband. Five husbands you have had, and the one you have now is not your husband—you have told the truth." The poor woman immediately acknowledged her sins ; she blushed and hung down her head, and said : " Good sir, I see that you are a prophet." She was now filled with reverential awe for Jesus—for she felt that He could see into her heart. But, at the same time, the extraordinary mildness of Jesus filled her with great confidence in Him. She next began to ask Him which was the true religion. Jesus explained all to her with the utmost simplicity, and finally told her that He Himself who was speaking to her was the long-expected Redeemer. The poor woman's joy was unbounded. She forgot to close the well, though it was strictly forbidden to leave it open—she forgot her jar of water—she could think only of the living water she had just discovered. She hastened back to the city, and cried aloud to all she met: "Come out to the well: I have found the Redeemer of the world." To confirm her words, she was not ashamed to cry out boldly: "I know that he is the Redeemer, for he has told me all my sins." This is one of the confessions which our divine Saviour heard Himself, in order to show us the necessity of confession.

Our Saviour not only heard confession Himself, but He also gave this divine power to His apostles. And it is fitting to remember here that this power of forgiving sins was given by God the Father to Jesus Christ, even as man. In the Gospel of St. Matthew, chapter xxviii. 18, we read that Jesus Christ said: "All power is given to me in heaven and on earth." By saying "all power in heaven and on earth is given to me," He plainly gives us to understand that He had also received from His heavenly Father the power of forgiving sins; and that He had this same power even as man is clearly implied in the words "is given to me." Had our Saviour when he uttered this considered Himself as God, He could not have said "is given to me," because as God He already had this power of Himself. He spoke as man, then, when He said "all power is given to me," and as man He could and did receive from His heavenly Father the power of forgiving sins. He even proved it by a miracle when some Scribes called this power of His into doubt. When the people brought to our Lord a man sick of the palsy, He said to the sick man: 'Son, be of good heart, thy sins are forgiven thee." Then some of the Scribes said within themselves, "He blasphemeth," thinking, as Protestants do, that God alone could forgive sins. But then our divine Saviour wishing to show them that He " even as man " had received power from His heavenly Father to forgive sins, wrought a great miracle in confirmation of this truth. He said : " But that you may know that the Son of Man has power on earth to forgive sins, then he saith to the man sick of the palsy, Arise, take up thy bed and go into thy house ; and he arose and went into his house, and the multitude seeing it feared and glorified God, who had given such power to men." *

Now this power which Jesus Christ as man had was again delegated by Him to other men, that is, to St. Peter and the rest of the apostles. This He did in the most solemn manner on the very day of His resurrection. On Easter Sunday night the apostles were assembled in the supper-room in Jerusalem. They had the doors and windows firmly barred and bolted, for they feared the Jews might break in on them and drag them to prison. Suddenly, Jesus Himself stood in their midst, and saluted them with the sweet words, " Peace be with you." The apostles were afraid, for they thought they saw a ghost. Jesus encouraged them and bade them touch Him: " See my hands and feet," He said, " it is I myself; feel and see ; a ghost has no flesh and bones as I." The apostles trembled with joy and wonder, and still hesitated. Jesus then told them to give Him something to eat, and He ate with them, and then they saw clearly that He was risen from the dead. Our divine Saviour now said to them: " Peace be with you. As the Father has sent me, I also send you ";† that is, with the same powers with which I, as man, am sent by my Father, I also send you as my delegates, as the pastors of my Church. And that there might not be the least doubt that in these words of His He included the power of forgiving sins, nay, to show in an especial manner that this power was included, He immediately breathed upon the apostles, and said to

Matt. ix. 2.   † John xx. 21.

them : " Receive ye the Holy Ghost : whose sins ye shall forgive, they are forgiven them; and whose sins you shall retain, they are retained." * Here, in the clearest terms,
Jesus Christ gives His apostles the power of forgiving sins,
in such a manner that when they here on earth exercise this
power by passing sentence of forgiveness over a penitent
sinner, their sentence is ratified in Heaven, and the sins of
the penitent are actually forgiven.

Mark well the words : " Whose sins you forgive, they
are forgiven them." No man who really loves the truth can
find any other meaning in these words than their plain
and natural meaning. Those words may be examined in
any grammar or dictionary of the English language, in any
language at all, in the Syro-Chaldaic, in the very language
our divine Saviour spoke ; and if we are sincere, we shall, we
can, find no other meaning in them than their natural and
obvious meaning : " Whose sins you forgive, they are forgiven them." What plainer words could our Saviour have
used, what other words could we ourselves use, to express the
fact that the apostles really received the power of forgiving
sins ?

Suppose the Emperor of Russia were to send an ambassador to this country, and, giving him full power to act as plenipotentiary, would say to him : " Whatsoever conditions
you agree to, I also agree to them ; and whatsoever conditions you reject, I also do reject them." Would not such
language be clear and explicit enough ? Would not every
one see that this ambassador was invested with the same
power as the emperor himself ? Now, this is precisely the
language of our divine Saviour to His apostles : " Whatsoever
sins you shall forgive, I also forgive them ; and whatsoever
sins you refuse to forgive, I also refuse to forgive them."

When God formed the first man out of the slime of the
earth, He breathed into his face the breath of life, and that

* John xx. 22.

instant man became a living soul, a living image of God. Now, also, God breathes upon His apostles the breath of life, and that very instant they became not merely images of God, for they were that already, but really Gods, as it were, having all power in heaven and on earth. "As the living Father hath sent me, so do I also send you." The heavenly Father had sent Jesus Christ to forgive sins, and to transmit this power to others, and Jesus in like manner sends His apostles with the power to forgive sins, and to transmit this power to their successors.

Our divine Saviour came on earth to forgive the sins of all men ; but He was not to live always here on earth, and, consequently, He had to leave this power to His successors, the apostles. The apostles, too, for the same reason, had to transmit this power to their successors, the bishops and priests, and this power must necessarily remain in the Church as long as there are sins to be forgiven.

The apostles clearly understood that they had received this divine power to forgive sins, and to transmit this power to their successors. In the Acts of the Apostles, as well as in their writings, we find express mention made of confession. St. Luke tells us that whilst the apostles were at Ephesus the faithful came and confessed their sins, and those who had been addicted to magic sciences brought their books together and burnt them publicly.* The Apostle St. John also tells us: "Let us confess our sins, for God is just and faithful." † God is just ; He requires a candid confession. God is faithful ; He will really pardon the sinner through the priest, as He has promised.

St. Paul the Apostle says expressly that he and the other apostles received from Christ the power of forgiving sins.‡ St. Clement, the disciple of St. Paul, whom St. Paul names in his Epistle, preached only what he had heard from St. Paul. This disciple speaks expressly of confession. He

* Acts xix. 18.   † 1 John i. 9.   ‡ 2 Cor. v. 18-20.

says that " in the other world neither confession nor penance will be of any avail." All the Fathers of the Church from the apostles down to our own day, speak of confession as a sacrament instituted by our Lord Jesus Christ Himself. All the older heretics and schismatics, without exception, the Armenians, the Copts, Greeks, Russians, have retained confession even to this day.

But nothing would seem better calculated to convince any one of the divine institution of confession, than its universal introduction and practice. It is a certain, undeniable fact that confession has always been practised from the time of the apostles down to the present day. Here, in America, it is practised in the North, in the South, in the East, and the West. Confession is practised in every country in Europe; it is practised in Asia, in Africa, and Australia; in the far-off islands of the Pacific. Everywhere, wherever a Catholic priest and a Catholic congregation are to be found, there is confession practised ; and it is not only practised but required under pain of eternal damnation. To confess is exceedingly contrary to flesh and blood ; to confess is most humbling to our pride, and most afflicting to our self-love. Most assuredly no human authority could have succeeded in laying so heavy a yoke and burden upon men. Human authority may succeed in abolishing confession in certain countries where it is practised. But no human authority could ever establish confession, making it a universal law all over the world. When the Protestants abolished confession in certain places of Germany, they soon perceived that the greatest disorders and licentiousness commenced to prevail, and that no one was any longer in security ; so they themselves requested the Emperor Charles V. to issue an edict which would oblige all to go to confession, " for," said they, " since confession has been abolished, it is impossible to live in peace with one another."

But the emperor knew that neither he nor any other hu

man authority was able to introduce confession, and that no human authority was able to establish confession, much less could any human authority maintain so difficult a precept. So he could not help laughing at such a request, and at the ignorance and stupidity of those who made it.

But suppose any human authority to have tried to introduce confession, who would have been the most violent opponents of this practice; who would have been the very first one to shake off this heavy burden? The Catholic bishops and priests. Why? Because they feel the pressure of this yoke and burden more than laymen. Not only are popes, bishops, and priests themselves to confess their sins, they are also bound to hear the confessions of others. What can be harder than this? How often must not the priest hazard his own health, his life, and even his immortal soul in order to hear the confession of some poor sinner! How often must the priest visit the plague-stricken in hospitals! How often must he remain for hours in a close room beside those infected with the most loathsome diseases? When St. Charles Borromeo was living, the pestilence broke out at Milan. More than one thousand priests died of it, because they assisted the plague-stricken and heard their confession. A few years ago a certain priest of this country was called to hear the confession of a dying person. The priest was unwell; he suffered from a violent fever; nevertheless, he went. He had to travel on foot for thirty miles to reach the dying person, and, after having administered to him the last Sacraments, he himself fell a corpse to the floor.

Now, could the Catholic priest bear such trials, could he brave such dangers, were the hand of God not with him? Would he suffer so much, and suffer it only in order to be able to assist and console his children, to hear their dying confessions, and to reconcile them to God—would he suffer all this did he not believe and know that confession is from God, did he not know that as priest of God he had the power of forgiving sins? But all those hardships which the Catholic priest must sometimes endure in the exercise of the sacred ministry, are but slight when compared to the interior trials, the trials of the soul, which he must often undergo precisely on account of confession. But the voice of the Lord must be obeyed. He commanded the apostles and their lawful successors to teach all nations. He commanded them to baptize all who would believe in their word. He told them that no one would enter into the kingdom of heaven without baptism. The same Lord gave power to the Apostles to forgive sins: " Whose sins you shall forgive, they are forgiven them." Let us praise and magnify the Lord for having given such power to man.

For outside the Church there is no remission of sins. She received as her very own the pledge of the Holy Spirit, without whom no sin whatever is remitted, so that those to whom sins are remitted receive life everlasting.

St. Augustine: *Enchiridion*, 65. (5th cent.)

ST. MATTHEW 9

6 But that you may know that the Son of man hath power on earth to forgive sins, (then said he to the man sick of the palsy): Arise, take up thy bed and go into thy house.

8 And the multitude seeing it, feared, and glorified God that gave such power to men.

CHAPTER VI.

TWO gentlemen went one day to visit a church in Paris. While examining its monuments and ornaments, their attention was attracted by a priest engaged in hearing confessions in one of the side chapels, and they began to laugh and joke at the expense of the penitent and confessor. "It is a laughable affair," said one of the gentlemen to his companion ; "I must amuse myself a little. Leave me for a short time ; we'll meet this evening at the theatre." "What do you mean to do ?" said the other. "Never mind," answered the first, "I wish to do something that shall afford you matter for amusement." So, leaving him, he went to examine some paintings till the priest came out of the confessional. When he came out, the gentleman followed him into the sacristy, and said : "Sir, I am thinking of going to confession, but let us go slowly about the business, if you please. You know, I presume, that men like me are not all saints; I, in particular, claim for myself a greater share of indulgence on your part than others, so as to make some equality between it and my faith, which, I assure you, is none of the strongest. I even wish you to begin by resolving certain difficulties, exaggerated perhaps by prejudice, but still sufficient to make me neglect, nay even hate and despise, confession." "You are, then, a Catholic ?" asked the priest. "Of course I am," answered he ; "I often even went to confession in my youth. But what I read, heard, and saw of confession has oeen more than sufficient to keep me away from it ; you can imagine

115

the rest yourself." "Easily," answered the priest; "but you have not succeeded equally well in finding out the way to overcome your prejudices. Confess your sins, sir, and you will soon change your opinion." "What, without previous explanations on the subject! I find a difficulty in bringing myself to do so ; I should first wish to see the necessity of confession proved." "Go to confession, sir, with a sincere resolution of changing your conduct, and you will have no more doubt on this subject than I have." "How! what do you mean ?" "That you have lost your faith by your bad conduct; you have judged ill of confession only after having abandoned yourself to vice."

The gentleman blushed, and after a moment's hesitation— "That is exactly the truth," said he, throwing himself into the arms of the priest—"that is exactly the truth ! How is it possible that I did not make that reflection myself ? I cannot go to confession to-day, as I came only with the intention of annoying you and insulting your ministry. Avenge yourself on my folly by becoming my conductor : I pledge my word of honor to come to you on whatever day you may appoint "; and he kept his promise.

After this first step all his prejudices vanished, and during the rest of his life he continued to think of confession like a Christian, because he lived like a Christian (*Soirées Villageoises*, vol. i.)

It is licentiousness alone that makes men object to and keeps them from confession. They who fly from it are assuredly never actuated by the desire of becoming more virtuous, but by the contrary desire of more freely gratifying their passions. The man of pure and chaste morals fears not the humble confession of his faults. The tree is known by its fruit ; and thus we never hear an upright, moral man speak badly of confession. Confession is one of nature's wants. Everything which is truly interior must be outwardly expressed. The love for Christ within us must manifest itself

116

externally in works of charity to the brethren, and what we do unto these we do to Him also. It is the same with contrition and the confession of sins before God, an act itself purely internal; if it be deep, strong, and energetic, it seeks an outward manifestation, and becomes the sacramental confession before the priest; and what we do to him we do again unto Christ likewise, whose place he represents.

Origen rightly compares sin to an indigestible food, which occasions sickness at the stomach, till it has been thrown off by a motion in the bowels. Ever so is the sinner tormented with internal pain, and he only enjoys quiet and full health when, by means of confession, he has, as it were, eased himself of the noxious internal stuff. The man who never opens his heart to any one, who never reveals his joys and his sorrows, who never discloses to a kindly friend the dark deeds that press so heavily on his conscience, is not to be trusted, and cannot be happy. Man is so constituted that he does not believe in his interior feelings unless he sees an outward manifestation of them, and, in fact, an internal sentiment is only ripened to consummation when it has acquired an outward shape. He therefore who truly and heartily hates sin, confesses it with an involuntary joyful pain ; with pain, because it is his own sin ; but with a joyful pain, because after confession it ceases to belong to him and to be his. This accounts for the well-known fact that criminals have often confessed their sins during sleep, or during a drunken or crazy fit, and many, unable to endure the remorse of conscience, have delivered themselves up to justice and confessed their sins publicly. And what are all the immoral books that now pollute society—the novels, the lewd poetry, and the rest—other than a public confession of the crimes and of the wicked lives of their authors ?

Very great, therefore, is the impious folly of Protestants who deny the necessity of confession. In spite of themselves, they have often involuntarily acknowledged the fact that confession is a want of the human heart.

The celebrated Cardinal Cheverus, who was formerly Bishop of Boston, was much beloved by Protestants as well as by Catholics, on account of his great learning and virtues. It often happened that even Protestant ladies of the most respectable families in Boston came to consult him. They told him their family troubles, their troubles of conscience, and asked his advice—precisely as Catholics do in confession. One day, a lady told the bishop that there was one doctrine of the Catholic Church which she disliked exceedingly, and which prevented her from becoming a Catholic, and this was the doctrine of confession. She could never prevail on herself to confess her sins : " Madam," answered the bishop smiling, " you say that you dislike confession, but your dislike is not so great as you imagine ; for to tell you the truth, you have been really confessing to me this long time. You must know that confession is nothing else than the confiding of your troubles and failings to a priest, in order to obtain his advice, and to receive through him the forgiveness of your sins."

What happened to this celebrated cardinal happens also to almost every priest. There are many noble-hearted souls created by God for a high purpose—to shine amid the angels throughout all eternity. Their sensibilities are so keen that they seem born only to suffer and weep. Their path to heaven is indeed a path of thorns. Their griefs and yearnings are such that but few can understand them. God help these noble souls if they are deprived of the strength and consolations of the Catholic Church ! Out of the Church they must bear their anguish alone. In the hour of happiness, they were told that religion would console them in the hour of sorrow. And now the hour of sorrow has come. Whither shall they turn for strength and consolation ? To books—to the Bible ? Books are cold and wearisome ; their words are dead. Oh ! how they envy the penitent Magdalen, who could sit at the feet of Jesus and hear from His blessed lips the sweet words of pardon and peace ! They turn to God in prayer, but God answers them not by the Urim and Thummim ; and, in their doubt and loneliness, they envy even the Jews of old. In vain do they listen for the voice of God, because God has appointed a voice to speak and answer in His name; but that voice is only within the shepherd's fold ; and they are kept without the fold by the cruel enemy, where the voice of the shepherd cannot reach them.

What are they to do to find relief ? Are they to apply to the Protestant minister ? An interior voice tells them to apply rather to a Catholic priest. The Rev. Father Bakewell tells us that, when a Protestant, he felt a strong desire to confess his sins. This desire grew stronger and stronger every day, so much so that he felt very unhappy because he could not satisfy it. One day the Protestant minister, who had a special affection for Mr. Bakewell, noticed that something unusual was troubling the mind of his young friend. So he called him and asked him the cause of his sadness. "Reverend sir," says Mr. Bakewell, "I want to go to confession." "Nonsense," replied the minister, with a sneer ; and then a discussion ensued between the minister and his disciple. The minister resorted to all sorts of arguments to dispel from Mr. Bakewell's mind what he termed Catholic notions, but all to no purpose. Mr. Bakewell was a man of sound judgment, and empty declamations could not satisfy him. Then, by an inconsistency which nothing could justify, the minister said to Mr. Bakewell: "Since you insist upon going to confession, the Book of Common Prayer declares that I have the power to hear you. I am ready." It was more than Mr. Bakewell could bear. "Sir," said he, "you have just told me that confession is absurd, contrary to the teaching of Christ, that it is priests' invention, a source of immorality, and now you expect to hear me ; permit me to say that I will never confess to a man who has no faith in confession—this looks too absurd ; I will apply to a priest, for he believes, and I do believe with him, that Christ has placed in his hands the twofold power of loosing and binding." A few days after, Mr. Bakewell was received into the bosom of the Church.

Now, what are these unsolicited manifestations of Protestants made to a Catholic priest ? Are they not an evident proof of the undeniable fact that confession is a want of nature ? Nay, even all our would-be infidels have ever been compelled to acknowledge this fact. Many of their emphatic avowals regarding the efficacy of confession might be adduced. Nay, many infidels have oftentimes, but especially at the hour of death, had recourse to this consoling sacrament. Mezerai, Toussaint, Maupertuis, De Boulainvilliers, La Mettrie, Dumarsais, D'Argens, Boulanger, De Tressan, De Laugle, Fontenelle, Buffon, Montesquieu, La Harpe, etc., went to confession before their death with all the sentiments of compunction and Christian piety. All the great standard-bearers of infidelity during the past century would have confessed their sins at their last hour had they not been hindered from so doing by their impious associates. Even D'Alembert himself expressed his desire of reconciling himself with his God. Condorcet, his friend, who shut out from the dying man the pastor of St. Germain, satanically congratulated himself upon such a triumph. " Oh !" said he, " were I not present, he would have flinched like the rest of them."

Diderot was in the best dispositions possible, he had frequent interviews with the parish priest of St. Sulpice, but his friends hastened to take him to the country, in order to save the philosophical body from the shame, as they called it, of his conversion. Voltaire went to confession during many of his attacks of sickness ; but not at his last hour, because his chamber-door was shut upon the chaplain of St. Sulpice, who was thus prevented from going to his bedside; and Voltaire died in such a terrible paroxysm of fury and rage that the Marshal of Richelieu, who was present at his cruel agony, exclaimed, "Really this sight is sickening, it is insupportable!" Listen to what his Protestant physician, M. Trochin, says of it : "Figure to yourself the rage and fury of Orestes, and you will still have but a feeble image of the fury of Voltaire in his last agony. It would be well if all the infidels of Paris were present. Oh ! the fine spectacle that would have met their eyes !"

But one may say : "Oh ! I am willing to confess my sins to God, but not to the Catholic priest." St. Thomas of Villanova answers: "As long as God was not made man, there was no strict command for man to confess his sins to man ; but since God became man, He has given all judgment to His Son, for He is appointed judge of the living and the dead ; and to Him, therefore, is man to render an account of his sins. But, because Christ has ascended to Heaven, He has delegated his priests to exercise that power, and He has declared in express terms that they have jurisdiction over sins to bind and to loose. And oh ! I wish you would understand what a great benefit and a great mercy this was." *   "Let no one say to me," says St. Augustine, "'I do penance in my heart, I confess all my sins to God and to God alone, who was present when I committed sin. It is He who must forgive me.' Then in vain was it said to the apostles, 'Whose sins you shall forgive they are forgiven them, and whose sins you shall retain they are retained !' Then the Church has received the keys to no purpose ; and so you make a mockery of the Gospel." To give the priest the power to forgive sins, and yet not to oblige any one to confess his sins to him, would indeed be to make a mockery of the priest. For how can the priest forgive a sin without know-

* Dom'nica III. Quæa.

ing it ? And how can he know the sin unless the sinner himself confesses it. In the sacrament of confession, the priest is a physician and judge. He is a physician, and consequently he must know the nature of the malady that afflicts the soul before he can cure it. He is a judge, and must consequently know what and how he has to judge.

What should we say of a judge who, without examining the cases brought before him, without questioning either the plaintiff or the defendant, would condemn at random one to be sent to prison, another to be hanged, and order another to be set at liberty ? Should we not think such a judge most unjust ? What, then, should we think of a priest who would absolve one and refuse to absolve another without asking any questions, without even listening to the penitent, but merely following his own blind caprices ? Would not such a priest be guilty of grievous injustice ? But it is precisely thus that every priest would be forced to act were Christians not strictly bound to confess all their sins to him.

As no one is foolish enough to say. " I will go to God and to God alone for the remission of original sin, I will send my children to God alone instead of sending them to the baptismal font," so, let no one be foolish enough to say, " I will go to God alone for the forgiveness of actual sin " ; for, as the former is forgiven only by means of baptism, so is the latter forgiven only by means of the sacrament of penance. Do all the good you can, distribute all you have among the poor, scourge yourself to blood every day, fast daily on bread and water, pray as long and as much as you are able, shed an ocean of tears on account of your sins—do all this, and yet if you have not the firm will to confess your sins, " you will," says St. Augustine, " be damned for not having been willing to confess them. Open therefore your lips, and confess your sins to the priest. Confession alone is the true gate to heaven."

122

St. Bonaventure relates that one of his brethren in religion was considered a saint by every one who knew him. He was seen praying in every place. He never spoke a word. In order not to be obliged to break silence, he made his confession only by signs. When St. Francis heard of this, he said: "Such conduct is no sign of sanctity. Know that this brother is a child of perdition. The devil has tied his tongue in order that he may not confess his sins in the manner he ought." The words of the saint were soon verified. This unhappy man soon after left the convent and died a bad death. For him, then, who has grievously sinned after baptism there is no other means left of obtaining God's pardon than by confessing his sins to the Catholic priest. This the devil, the great enemy of our salvation, knows well—hence his artifices to keep men from confession. When the Prodigal Son arose at last to return to his loving father, the tempter stood beside him and said: "What are you doing? You cannot go back to your father in that plight. You are all in rags. Your father will be ashamed of you. He will not own you. Besides, the distance is too great. You will lose your way. You will be attacked by robbers and wild beasts. Moreover, you are now too weak and sickly, you will faint and die on the way. Wait yet a few days longer. This famine will not last always. You will have better times by and by. If you go back to your father, you will be scolded and treated even more harshly than before. If you go back now, every one will say that you are a coward—every one will laugh at you." How cunning and crafty is Satan! It is thus that this infernal spirit always tries to keep the poor sinner from returning to God, his heavenly Father.

There is a man who is not yet a Catholic, though inclined to become one. The devil makes him believe that confession is not a divine institution, but an invention of men; that it is even blasphemous to say and believe that man can forgive sins; that confession is too difficult a duty for man to perform, and that therefore a God of infinite kindness could not oblige man to perform it ; that a secret confession made to Him alone is all that is required. There is a Catholic who has stayed away from confession for thirty, forty, or fifty years. He makes up his mind at last to go to confession. Then comes the devil and whispers in his ear : " Oh ! there is no hope for you. You have stayed away too long from confession. Your sins are too great and too numerous. You cannot obtain forgiveness. Besides, you will never be able to remember all of them. It is useless for you to go to confession."

There is a young woman who has been leading a worldly life. She has been keeping dangerous company. She has permitted sinful liberties. She sometimes reads senti-mental novels and weekly magazines. She hears a sermon ; her conscience is aroused ; and she wishes to make a good confession. But the devil comes to her and says : " What are you going to do ? The priests are too strict. Do not go near them. They will make you promise a great many things ; and then after the confession you will break your promises, and you will be worse than before."

There is another unhappy soul. She has been for years making bad confessions and sacrilegious communions. At last she wishes to make a good confession, to tell everything that is on her conscience ; but the devil comes and whispers in her ear : " Oh ! what will the priest think of you if you tell these horrid sins ? The priest never heard such sins before. He will be horrified—he will scold you." In using such artifices to keep men from confession, the devil is like to Holofernes besieging Bethulia. Seeing that he could not take the city by main force, Holofernes destroyed all the water-conduits. Thus the inhabitants, for want of water saw themselves forced to surrender. The devil knows that the sacrament of penance is the only happy channel through

124

which the divine grace of reconciliation flows upon the sinner. He knows that the sinner remains in his power if he succeeds either in making him not believe in the necessity of confession, or in inducing him to stay away from it, or to make a bad confession. The devil knows well how true are the words of our Saviour : " Whose sins you shall retain, they are retained "—that is, they will not be forgiven for all eternity. How many souls are now burning in hell for not having believed in the necessity of confession, for having put off confession too long, or for having made bad confessions !

The Rev. Father Furniss, C.SS.R., relates that there was a certain gentleman living in the North of England, in Yorkshire. He led a very wicked life, and knew that those who lead wicked lives deserve to go to hell. He wanted to be bad during his lifetime, and still not go to hell when he died. So he began to think how he might gratify his passions and still save himself from hell after all. He thought that he had found out a way to save his soul after leading a bad life. When I am dying, he thought, I will repent and send for the priest, and make my confession, and then all will be right. But then he remembered that if he had to send for the priest when he was dying, perhaps the priest might not be at home ; or perhaps his illness might be very short, and the priest could not come soon enough to hear his confession. He was frightened when he remembered that he might die before the priest could arrive. So he thought of another plan. He would get a priest to come and live always in the house with him, so that at any moment he could send for the priest. This thought pleased him very much, for he felt sure that if a priest was always living in his house he should be quite safe. But he forgot those words, " As people live, so shall they die." He forgot that he was offending God very much, and that, after all, how we shall die depends entirely on God.

125

A year or two after this his last illness came, and it came upon him very suddenly, when he was not expecting it. He felt that he was dying, so he told his servants to go and fetch the priest to hear his confession. The priest was in the house, and the servants went directly to find him. They went first of all to the priest's own room, which was next to the room in which the gentleman lay dying. The servants, not finding the priest in his own room, went through the whole house, from the highest to the lowest room, but could not find him anywhere. They called out his name all over the house, but there was no answer to their call. So they went back to their master, and told him that the priest was nowhere to be found. Then the gentleman saw how he had been deceiving himself, despair came into his heart, and he died without hope of salvation.

A few moments after he had died the servants happened to go again into the priest's room, and there they saw the priest reading the prayers in his office-book. "How long," they said, "has your reverence been here?" "I have been here all the morning." "Did you not go out of the room any time?" "No," said the priest, "I have not been out for one moment." "Did you not then see us come into this room two or three times, or hear us calling out your name?" "No," said the priest, "I did not see any one come into this room, or hear any one call out my name." "As people live, so they die."

If we have followed the Prodigal Son in his sins, let us follow him now in his repentance. The Prodigal Son made up his mind to return to his father, no matter what it would cost. He was sorry for what he had done, and was determined to make reparation to the best of his power. No evil companion, no suggestion of the devil, could prevail upon him to stay any longer in a strange country—in a state of mortal sin. He was determined to make his confession to his father and obtain forgiveness. We, too, must show such determination, and say to ourselves : No matter what it may cost me; no matter what the neighbors may say ; no matter what my friends may say, I am determined with God's help to make a good confession and to give up this life of sin.

Let us be wise, and let us be wise in time—that is, let us confess our sins in time, for in the world to come there is no one to hear our confession and give us absolution ; not even the apostles can do so. It is only in this world that we can find a created being who has power to forgive the sinner, who can free him from the chains of sin and hell ; and that extraordinary being is the *priest*, the Catholic priest. " Who can forgive sins except God ? " was the question which the Pharisees sneeringly asked. " Who can forgive sins ?" is the question which the Pharisees of the present day also ask ; and the answer is, There *is* a man on earth that can forgive sins, and *that* man is the Catholic priest.

And not only does the priest declare that the sinner is forgiven, but he *really forgives* him. The priest raises his hand, he pronounces the words of absolution, and in an instant, quick as a flash of light, the chains of hell are burst asunder, and the sinner becomes a child of God. So great is the power of the priest that the judgments of Heaven itself are subject to his decision ; the priest absolves on earth, and God absolves in Heaven. "Whatsoever you shall bind on earth, shall be bound in Heaven ; and whatsoever you shall loose on earth, shall be loosed also in Heaven " (Matt. xviii. 18). These are the ever-memorable words which Jesus Christ addressed to the apostles and to their successors in the priesthood.

Suppose that our Saviour Himself were to come down from Heaven, and were to appear here in our midst ; suppose He were to enter one of the confessionals to hear confessions. Now, let a priest enter another confessional, for the same purpose. Suppose that two sinners go to confession, both equally well disposed, equally contrite. Let one of these go to the priest, and the other to our Saviour Himself. Our Lord Jesus Christ says to the sinner that comes to Him : " I absolve thee from thy sins " ; and the priest says to the sinner that goes to him : "I absolve thee from thy sins " ; and the absolution of the priest will be just as valid, just as powerful, as the absolution of Jesus Christ Himself.

At the end of the world Jesus Christ will Himself judge all men; " for the Father judges no one, but He has left all judgment to his divine Son." But as long as this world lasts, Jesus Christ has left all judgment to His priests. He has vested them with His own authority, with His own power. " He that heareth you," He says, " heareth me." He has given them His own divine Spirit. " Receive ye the Holy Ghost · whosesoever sins you shall forgive, they are forgiven ; and whosesoever sins you shall retain, they are retained."

The priest is the ambassador, the plenipotentiary of God. He is the co-operator, the assistant, of God in the work of redemption. This is no exaggeration, it is the inspired language of the apostle : " Dei adjutores sumus." * " We are the co-operators, the assistants, of God." It is to the priest that God speaks when He says, "Judge between me and my people "—" Judica inter me et vineam meam." † " This man," says God, speaking to the priest, "is a sinner ; he has offended me grievously ; I could judge him myself, but I leave this judgment to your decision. I will forgive him as soon as you grant him forgiveness. He is my enemy, but I will admit him to my friendship as soon as you declare him worthy. I will open the gates of Heaven to him as soon as you free him from the chains of sin and hell."

There lived in the city of Antwerp, in Belgium, a certain nobleman who had, in his youth, the misfortune to fall into a very grievous sin. Day and night his conscience tortured

* 1 Cor. iil.

† Isa. v.

him, but yet he could not prevail upon himself to confess this sin; death, even hell itself, did not seem to him so terrible as such a confession. One day he was present at a sermon which gave him much consolation. The priest said, among other things, that "one is not obliged to confess those sins which he has entirely forgotten." The nobleman now did all in his power to forget this sin. He was rich and so he cast himself into the whirl of gay amusements— every pleasure, lawful and unlawful, was enjoyed ; he sought to bury his sin beneath a mountain of new sins ; but all in vain ! Far above the sweet music, far above the gay song and the merry laugh, louder than all, rose the voice of his conscience, and amidst the gayest crowds he carried a hell in his heart.

He now tried another plan. He began to travel. He travelled over many lands; he saw everything that was quaint or beautiful. A change of climate, he thought, would bring about a change of heart; but he was sadly disappointed. Every day he saw new sights ; without everything was new and changing, but within—in his soul—was ever that dead, dreary sameness, for he carried himself with him everywhere—everywhere that wicked deed haunted him. The blue skies and the sunny lands smiled not for him; his guilty conscience cast a gloomy shadow on all he beheld. Weary and heart-sick, he returned to his native city.

He there applied himself earnestly to study, and thought to beguile his soul into forgetfulness. He dived into the abstractions of mathematics and philosophy, he soared aloft and calculated the courses of the stars, he listened to the lectures of the most learned professors ; but all in vain. Every book he opened seemed to tell him of his sin. The voice of his professor sounded in his ear, but far louder deep down in his soul, sounded the voice of his conscience.

The unhappy man was at last almost driven to despair

Another sermon, however, gave him new courage. He heard that " charity covereth a multitude of sins," "that God can never despise a contrite and humble heart." He heard that good works, alms-deeds, as also perfect contrition, obtain from God the forgiveness of our sins. He now applied himself with all the fervor of his soul to the practice of good works. He spent whole nights in prayer, he fasted long and frequently, he performed the most rigorous penances, he bestowed liberal alms on the poor, he visited prisons and the hospitals, he assisted and consoled the suffering and dying ; but though he consoled many and many a one, there was no consolation for himself. Every moment his conscience upbraided him: " You must do the one, and the other you must not omit " ; you must do good works, but you must also confess your sins !

The unhappy nobleman had now tried all that man could do, had tried every means but the only right one, and had tried all in vain. There was but one resource left. He was weary of life, and was resolved to end it by suicide. He stepped into his carriage and drove off to his country-seat. As he passed along the road he overtook a venerable old man, whom he recognized as a religious priest. The nobleman immediately stopped his carriage and invited the aged priest to enter. The priest, in order to please the nobleman, yielded to his request. The good old father was very friendly and talkative. They spoke of various things, and the conversation soon turned upon religious matters. The priest spoke at length of the clearly-distinctive notes of the Holy Catholic Church. He spoke with a joyous pride of her holy Sacraments, especially of that most touching proof of God's infinite mercy—the holy Sacrament of Confession. " What hope could there be for the poor sinner," cried he, with enthusiasm—" what hope could there be were it not for confession ? Yes, yes, confession is the last plank after shipwreck ; confession is the sinner's last and only hope of salvation." At these words the nobleman started up as if stung by a serpent. "What!" cried he, "what is that you say? Do you know me? How do you know me?" The priest was quite astonished by this sudden outburst, and excused himself, saying: "My dear sir, I have never before had the honor of knowing you. If I have inadvertently said anything to wound your feelings, you must excuse me. Old people, you know, are generally talkative. However, if you should have any troubles of conscience, you may be sure I would be only too happy to assist you." "But," cried the nobleman, excited, "what if I do not wish to confess?" "Oh! then," said the priest, quietly, "if you do not wish to confess, why then—never mind it. You know there are other means." These last words fell as a ray of sunshine upon the dreary and clouded soul of the nobleman. "There are other means," thought he, and he began to breathe again freely once more. He now felt the greatest confidence in the good old priest, promised him solemnly that he would be willing to undergo every penance if he could only be relieved from the objection of going to confession. They soon arrived at the country-seat, and the priest was obliged to stay over night. They passed the evening in agreeable conversation. The hour for retiring came, but the nobleman would not suffer the priest to retire to rest until he revealed to him those "other means" of which he had spoken. The priest now advised him to remain awake yet for a few hours to enliven his confidence in God, and to examine his conscience carefully. "Not, of course," said he, "in order to confess, for that you do not wish to do, but that you may call to mind all your sins, and be truly sorry for them. To-morrow morning I will tell you the rest."

You may imagine that the nobleman slept little that night. Early the next morning he was at the priest's door. "I have complied faithfully with your injunctions," said he. " What have I to do next ? " " Oh ! all you have to do now," answered the priest, smiling, " is to come with me into the garden." They stepped forth into the cool morning air. "Well, how are you," said the priest, in a kind tone. " Do you not feel better ? " " Better !" answered the nobleman, "oh ! no ; far from it." " But," said the priest, "perhaps you forgot something in your examen of conscience. Did you think of this sin, and this, and this? " And so he went on gradually through the long train of sins of which the human heart is capable. He descended into the deepest depths of human degradation, and named even those sins that are so dark and shameful that one is afraid to acknowledge them to himself.

Scarcely had the good priest named a certain sin when the nobleman became greatly agitated. He hid his face in his hands and sobbed aloud. "Yes ! That's it ! That's it ! That is the abominable, the accursed sin that I cannot —that I will not confess." The priest could not help weeping at witnessing the struggle of this poor soul. He consoled the nobleman, and told him that there was no need of confessing it any more. " You have confessed already," said he ; " let it now be forgotten. You can include whatever other sins you remember, and now kneel down and receive the absolution." The nobleman fell on his knees and wept like a child. He kissed again and again the hand of the aged priest, and arose with a heart as light as if he had that of an angel who never knew aught of sin. He felt as if he stood in a new creation. Never before did the sun shine so brightly ; never before did the heavens look so blue ; never before did the birds sing so sweetly. His happiness was as a foretaste of heaven.

If we have followed the Prodigal in his sinful career, let us now follow him also in his good confession. Let us say with him. "I will go to my father and say to him : father I have sinned against Heaven and before thee. I am no more worthy to be called thy son " ; * and our heavenly Father will receive us again into His grace and friendship. He will look upon us again as His children, and say to His angels : " Behold this poor sinner, he was dead and is come to life again, he was lost and is found."   " Confession is the gate to heaven " †

* Luke xv. 18, 19.   † St. Augustine.

With good reason does Peter, out of all the apostles, act in the person of the Catholic Church—for to this Church were the keys of the kingdom of heaven given when bestowed on Peter (Matth., 16, 19). Hence when the Lord asked him: *Dost thou love Me?* (John, 21, 15) that question was put to all. The Catholic Church, then, ought readily to pardon her children when they repent and are re-established in devotion to her.

St. Augustine: *De Agone Christiano,* 32. (4th cent.)

133

CHAPTER VII.

A FAMOUS missionary in Italy was one day preaching to an immense multitude. He stood in the open air, under the clear blue sky, and the wide field around him was thronged with the thousands who had come to hear him. It was summer, and the lofty trees around with their rich foliage made an agreeable shade to the audience. A dead silence fell upon all, and all eyes were riveted upon the speaker. There he stood, his arms extended, his eyes raised to heaven; he was rapt in ecstasy. A moment more and the missionary broke the solemn stillness, and cried aloud in a voice so strong and awful that it caused the ears of his hearers to tingle, and penetrated the very marrow of their bones: "Oh! my brethren, how many, many souls are damned. Just now God opened my eyes, and I saw the souls of men falling into hell as the dead leaves fall in the harvest-time." And, lo! as he spoke, a mighty wind there arose, and the green leaves dropped from the trees though it was yet summer, and the earth was strewn with the fallen leaves, and all who heard him were filled with unspeakable terror.

Were God to open our eyes this moment, we would also see how the souls of men even now are falling into hell thick as the snow-flakes fall in winter. Did not the Son of God come on earth to save all men? Did not the Blessed Jesus pour out the last drop of his heart's blood to rescue all men from hell? Did he not make the way to heaven so easy that all we have to do to be saved is to will it earnestly?

134

This is all most true, and yet even now the souls of men are falling into hell. And why? There is scarcely one in the world who has never committed a sin ; and there are few, very few who have never committed a mortal sin ; and there are millions who never confess their sins, never repent of them ; and millions again who confess them, indeed, but who do not confess them all, or who do not confess them in a manner as they ought.

In order to obtain the forgiveness of our sins in confession, the confession must be like that of the Prodigal Son His confession was humble. "Father," he said, "I am not now worthy to be called thy son, for I have sinned against Heaven and before thee." Our confession must always be humble, for in being humble it will always be entire ; that is, no mortal sin will be purposely omitted or concealed. He who is truly sorry for his sins is most willing to confess them all ; he is even apt to confess them more minutely than is necessary. Integrity of confession is required for eternal salvation ; for any deadly sin purposely omitted will never be blotted out of the soul. Should a dastardly fear and a misplaced shame withhold any one from making known to his confessor a single mortal sin, he will, on this account alone, remain under God's displeasure, and in danger of eternal perdition.

There are many instances of this. A young person of eighteen, who lived in Florence, in Italy, had the misfortune to fall into temptation and commit a great sin. No sooner had she done so than she found herself covered with confusion and torn with remorse. "Oh !" said she to herself, "how shall I have the courage to declare that sin to my confessor ? What will he think of me ? What will he say to me ?" She went, nevertheless, to confession, but dared not confess that sin. She got absolution, and had the misfortune to receive communion in that state. This horrible sacrilege increased still more her remorse and trouble.

She was, as it were, in hell, tormented day and night by the reproaches of her conscience, and by the well-founded fear of being lost for ever. In the hope of quieting ner conscience, she gave herself up to tears and groans, to continual prayer, to the most rigorous fasts and to the hardest privations ; but all was in vain. The remembrance of her first crime and her sacrileges harassed and pursued her incessantly. Her soul was, as it were, in an abyss of sorrow and bitterness. In the height of her interior anguish a thought came into her mind to go into a convent and make a general confession, in which it would be easy for her to declare her sin. She did so, and commenced the confession she had proposed making; but still enslaved by false shame, she related the hidden sin in such a garbled, confused way that her confessor did not understand it, and yet she continued to receive communion in that sad state. Her trouble became so great that life appeared insupportable. To relieve her heart, tormented as it was, she redoubled her prayers, mortifications, and good works to such an extent that the nuns in the convent took her for a saint, and elected her for their superior. Become superior, this wretched hypocrite continued to lead outwardly a penitential and exemplary life, embittered still by the reproaches of her conscience. To moderate her horrible fears a little, she at length made a firm resolution to confess her sin in her last illness, which came sooner than she expected. Then she immediately undertook a general confession, with the good intention of confessing the sin she had always concealed ; but shame restrained her more strongly than ever, and she did not accuse herself of it. She still consoled herself with the thought that she would declare it a few moments before her death ; but neither the time nor the power to do so was given her. The fever rose so high that she became delirious, and so died. Some days after, the religious of the monastery being in prayer for the repose of the soul of this pretended saint, she appeared to them in a hideous form, and told them. "Sisters, pray not for me; it is useless. I am damned!" "How?" cried an old religious; "you are damned after leading such a holy and penitential life! Is it possible?" "Alas! yes. I am damned for having all my life concealed in confession a mortal sin which I committed at the age of eighteen years." Having said this she disappeared, leaving behind her an intolerable stench, the visible sign of the sad state in which she was. This story is related by St. Antoninus, Archbishop of Florence, who wrote in the fifteenth century.*

Such then is the melancholy end of all those who conceal their sins in confession and die in that state. They suffer a hell in this world, as well as in that to come.

The sinner says, "I feel so much ashamed, I cannot confess my sins." If the confession were made to an angel, a bright and beautiful spirit from heaven, then indeed might one hesitate, and feel afraid and ashamed to tell all his shameful secret sins to a spirit so pure, so holy. Not to an angel, however, have we to confess, but to a poor sinful mortal like ourselves; to a fellow-creature subject to temptation like ourselves; to one who stands in need of the grace of God as much as we do; to one, perhaps, who stands more in need of God's grace than we do, for his duties, his responsibilities, his dangers are far greater. Why then should we be afraid to tell our sins to the priest? What is there in the priest that should cause fear in us? Shame? Is it not better to suffer a little shame now than to endure unutterable shame on the day of judgment and eternal shame in hell?

Tertullian, who lived in the second century, said: "There are many Christians who are ashamed to confess their sins, thinking more about their shame and confusion than about their salvation. Though we hide something

* Abbé Favre, *Le Ciel Ouvert*, 45.

from men, can we hide it also from God ? Which is better : to be damned for having concealed our sins, or to be saved for having confessed them ? "

One day a certain priest saw the devil standing at the confessional. He asked him what he was doing there. " I make restitution," answered the devil ; " I give back to the sinner the shame which I took from him when about to commit sin." This is always a very successful trick of the devil. When he sees any one about to commit sin, he takes away from him all fear and shame ; but as soon as he nas committed it, the devil gives him back all the fear and shame he had taken from him, and thus throws the unhappy soul into despair.

When the wolf wishes to carry off a lamb, he seizes his helpless victim by the throat, so that it cannot warn the shepherd, and cannot cry for help. It is thus that the infernal wolf, the devil, acts with souls. He is afraid that they will tell their sins and thereby escape from his clutches ; ne therefore holds them by the throat, so that they cannot make a full and candid confession.

" Remark," says St. Anthony of Padua, "that through many chambers can the demon have access to the house of our conscience—that is, our mind—but that only through one door can he be expelled, that is, through the mouth, by confession. He can enter by the five senses, but only by the lips can he be ejected. When, therefore, the demon has obtained possession of this castle, the first thing he does is to block up the way by which he could be driven out— that is, he makes man mute ; for with this door closed he feels secure in his possession.*

Sin and obstinacy tie the tongues of many sinners. We read in the *Magnum Speculum* that a person possessed by the devil was led to a holy man, to whose questions the demon said : " We are three within him ; I am called *Clau-*

* Dominica iii. in Quad

dens Cor (the closer of the heart) ; my office is to prevent men from having contrition ; but if I fail, then my brother, called *Claudens Os* (the closer of the mouth), endeavors to prevent him from confessing his sins; but if he confesses and is converted, my third brother here, named *Claudens Bursam* (the closer of the purse), labors to prevent him from making restitution, filling his mind with the fear of poverty; and he succeeds more frequently than either of us."

The famous Socrates was one day going along the street, and happening to pass a house of ill fame, he saw the door open and one of his own disciples coming out. As the young man beheld Socrates, he was filled with shame and went back into the house. But Socrates went to the door and called him : "My son," said he, "leave this house instantly, and know that it is indeed a disgrace to enter such a house, but it is an honor to leave it." What Socrates said to his frail disciple is wholesome advice for Christians. It is indeed a shame, a dishonor, to commit sin ; but it is a glory, an honor, to confess it. By sin we become enemies of God and slaves of the devil, but by confession we again become children of God and heirs of heaven.

Suppose we were afflicted with a very dangerous cancer ; should we be ashamed to go to the physician and tell him about it ? Would we not suffer him even to probe the painful wound ? Certainly we would; and why ? Because life is very dear to us, and we are willing to endure the greatest pain and the greatest humiliation rather than lose our life. And shall we not suffer a little pain, a little humiliation, to save our immortal soul ? Can we not endure a little shame in order to free our soul from the horrible cancer of mortal sin ?

Suppose we owed a hundred millions of dollars to a king. But the king being moved with pity, forgives us the whole debt on condition that we go to one of his ministers to acknowledge this immense debt, upon which acknowledg ment the minister is to give us a receipt of payment. Should we not feel only too happy to pay off our great debt on so easy a condition ? Should we not go at once and comply most cheerfully with such a condition ?

But do we not know how great a debt we have contracted with Almighty God by a mortal sin ? This is a debt which all the money of the world, all the saints in heaven, all the good works of the just on earth, are not sufficient to cancel ; nay, even the fierce fires of hell, though burning throughout all eternity, can never destroy a single mortal sin. It is a debt which makes us so hideous in the sight of God that, could we be permitted to enter with it into heaven, we should at once empty that beautiful abode of eternal bliss of all its angels and saints. See then how good the Lord is. To pay off this debt, and to obtain a receipt for it, all that He requires of us is to go to a lawful minister of His—to a priest—and acknowledge to him the full amount of our debt. Can that condition be too hard which affords us an opportunity to escape hell ? Indeed God has shown Himself extremely indulgent on this point. He could certainly have made a far more difficult condition as the means of obtaining pardon, as the only path to salvation and the only plank left after shipwreck.

Confession is the great, the wonderful institution of the infinite mercy of God. There have been many sinners who have entered the confessional without the least intention of changing their conduct ; many even have entered for no other purpose than to mock the priest and ridicule this divine institution ; but they went away quite changed. They entered as wolves and left as lambs.

The good priest spoke to them kindly, his heart was touched with pity for them ; he made them enter into themselves and reconciled them with their God.

It is related of St. Alphonsus that he never sent away a sinner without giving him absolution. Now, it is morally certain that many a sinner came to him who was not disposed to receive absolution. But then the great saint spoke to the poor sinner with the utmost kindness; he represented to him in forcible language the miserable condition of his soul, and the great danger of eternal damnation; he inspired him with a salutary fear of the judgments of God, and at the same time prayed hard and with tears in his eyes to Jesus in the Blessed Sacrament, and to the Blessed Virgin Mary, to obtain for the sinner that change of heart and that sorrow which disposed him for the forgiveness of his sins, for the worthy reception of the sacrament of penance. Go, then, to confession, and go without fear; ask the priest to be kind enough to help you make a good confession. If you experience a particular difficulty in confessing a certain sin, tell your confessor of the difficulty, and he, in his kindness, will make all easy for you. All that is necessary to be done is to answer his questions with true sincerity of heart.

Suppose you fell into a deep pit, filled with fierce, venomous serpents, would you be ashamed to take hold of the rope which a friend let down in order to draw you out of the horrible place? Would you not seize the rope with eagerness? Would you not be for ever thankful to the friend who had delivered you from the poisonous fangs of the serpents? Most certainly you would. And have you no thanks to offer your best and truest friend, the priest of God? Will you not suffer him to deliver you from the poisonous fangs of the hellish serpents, that have been so long swarming in your soul? Will you not suffer the priest to free you from the power of those demons of hell, that for years have been haunting you, have been tempting and tormenting you day and night, sleeping and waking? Will you not suffer the priest to free you from the devils, who are ever trying so hard to deprive you of the glory and joys of heaven, to drag you, with them, deep down into the flames of hell?

"But oh !" you will say, "if I tell such a sin the priest will be scandalized and horrified. I am sure he never before heard such dreadful sins as mine. What will he think of me ?"

What ! the priest will be scandalized ? Did you ever know of a physician being scandalized or offended at a patient for being very sick ? Why, the very fact of his being sick is precisely the reason why the physician comes to him. If he were well, he would not need the physician. The priest is the physician of the soul, and it is precisely because the soul is sick that you stand so much in need of his assistance. A father feels more compassion for a sick child than for one that is well.

"The priest never heard such sins before." That is unfortunately a sad mistake. The priest must study for many long years to prepare himself for the sacred ministry. Before he is ever permitted to enter the confessional, he must study for years in moral theology every possible sin that man can commit. He must study his own heart, and the knowledge of his own heart gives him an insight into the hearts of his fellow-men. He knows from his own experience how strong are the human passions, how weak the human heart. He knows every fold of the heart ; its most secret desires, its hidden weakness, its natural tendency to evil. The priest has had, moreover, a long experience in hearing confessions. It is his duty often to probe the inmost recesses of his heart ; he has to become acquainted with sin in its most hideous and revolting forms. There is little reason to fear that the priest will be astonished at what is told him ; and if he should seem astonished, it is not so much at the sins which the sinner confesses as that he has not fallen into even greater sins.

You say, "If I tell such a shameful sin, what will the priest think of me ? He will have a bad opinion of me." The priest will honor you for your courage if you make a frank, honest confession. It is certain that it requires more courage to make a clear, candid confession than it does to brave death upon the battle field. The courage of the soldier on the battle-field is a mere animal courage. The horse and the mule, too, rush headlong into the very jaws of death ; but the courage of him that confesses even his most secret sins is moral courage, it is sterling virtue. Men who brave death on the battle-field display in that action less real moral courage than a little school-girl does who goes to confession ; they had not courage enough to go to confession; they were cowards, they dared not. Many a young man who thinks himself very brave, and who would be insulted if you called him a coward, is a coward who dares not go to confession.

The priest will honor the sincere penitent, he will esteem him, he will even love him ; for, by making a candid confession, he has become a child of God and an heir of heaven ; and after confession the soul becomes bright and beautiful as an angel of God.

At the close of a mission where St. Francis de Sales had spent day and night in hearing confessions, he wrote to St. Jane Frances de Chantal as follows : " Oh ! how great is my joy over the conversion of so many souls. I have been reaping in smiles and in tears of love amongst my dear penitents. O Saviour of my soul ! how great was my joy to see, among others, a young man of twenty, brave and stout as a giant, return to the Catholic faith, and confess his sins in so holy a manner that it was easy to recognize the wonderful workings of divine grace leading him back to the way of salvation. I was quite beside myself with joy."

Another time a great sinner brought himself with much repugnance to make a general confession to St. Francis de Sales, in which he detailed the many sins of his youth. The saint, charmed by the great humility with which the penitent went through the painful task of confessing his sins

143

expressed to him his joy and satisfaction. "You wish to console me," said the penitent, "because you cannot esteem such a guilty creature as I am." "You are mistaken," answered the saintly bishop; "I would be a perfect Pharisee were I to look upon you as a sinner after absolution. At the present moment your soul is, in my estimation, whiter than snow, and I am bound to love you for two reasons—the first, because of the confidence you have shown me by candidly opening your heart to me ; and the second, because, being the instrument of your birth in Jesus Christ, you are my son. And as to my esteem for you, it equals the love that I bear you. By a miracle of the right hand of God, I see you transformed from a vessel of ignominy to a vessel of honor and sanctification. Moreover, I should indeed be very insensible did I not participate in the joy that the angels themselves feel on account of the change wrought in your heart; how I love that heart which now loves the God of all goodness !" The penitent went away so satisfied that ever after his greatest delight was to go to confession.* Such is the joy and love of every priest for and over every poor sinner who has sincerely confessed his sins.

But you will say: "Oh ! if I tell such horrid sins, the priest will scold me." Could you but look into the priest's heart, you would not judge him so harshly. The priest is indeed an enemy of sin, but he is the truest friend of the sinner. The priest knows very well how much it costs to make a confession. How often has your wife, or your mother, or your sister, or some kind friend, entreated and even scolded you before you would consent to go to confession. How often has your conscience warned and terrified you before you would consent to confess. The priest knows all this very well. He knows, too, how often you made up your mind to go to confession, how you lost courage and put the confession off till some other time. He knows all

* *Spirit of St. Francis de Sales.*

144

the enquiries you made, all the pains you took to find out an easy confessor, one who would not be too hard on you. The priest knows also how much time you spent in preparing for confession, in waiting for your turn at the confessional; how you lost thereby a good day's work, and were even in danger of losing your employment. The priest knows of all your sacrifices and struggles; and do you think he will scold you or treat you harshly when you come to him in spite of all these obstacles? Oh! no. The priest knows from his own experience how much it costs to make a full and candid confession. He is a man like yourself, he has a human heart, human weaknesses, temptations like yourself. He too has to cast himself at the feet of a brother priest for confession.

Our divine Saviour assures us that the angels of heaven rejoice over one who gives up sin and enters upon a life of penance. He says that there is even more joy in heaven over one sinner doing penance than over ninety-nine just who need not penance. If the angels of heaven rejoice when you come repentant to confession, will not the heart of the priest rejoice when he sees you humbly kneeling before him? As the heart of a mother rejoices on finding her long-lost child, so does the heart of the priest rejoice when he sees the poor lost prodigal returning home at last.

"Oh!" you will say, "but perhaps the priest will speak of my sins, and reveal them to others."

Suppose you were to confess your sins to the wall, would you be afraid that your sins would be revealed? You may be just as certain that the sins you tell the priest will never be revealed. The priest is bound by the most sacred, the most solemn obligations—he is bound by every law, natural, ecclesiastical, and divine—to observe the utmost secrecy with regard to every sin and imperfection revealed to him. He is not allowed to speak of your sins out of confession, even to yourself, unless you give him permission to do so. So

145

strict is the obligation of the seal of confession that could the priest release all the damned souls in hell by revealing a single sin he heard in confession, he would not be permitted to do so. Nay, he must even suffer imprisonment and death—he must be willing to endure every torment—rather than break the seal of confession.

One of the greatest monsters that ever sat on a throne was Wenceslaus IV., King of Bohemia. So great were his debaucheries that he was generally called by his subjects "Wenceslaus the drunkard." As is always the case with wicked men, he became jealous of his wife. Being resolved to find out whether his suspicions were well grounded, he sent for the confessor of the queen. This confessor was the holy priest, St. John Nepomuck. The tyrant commanded the priest to reveal all that the queen had confessed to him. St. John answered firmly that such a thing was utterly impossible. The emperor tried to win the saint by rich presents; but the confessor spurned such a sacrilegious proposal. The emperor threatened him with imprisonment and death. The confessor answered: "I can die, but I cannot break the seal of confession." The tyrant ordered him to be put to the torture. The holy confessor was stretched on the rack, burning torches were applied to his side, he was commanded to reveal the secrets; but he only raised his eyes to heaven and repeated again and again the sweet names of Jesus and Mary. The tyrant, furious at seeing himself thus baffled, ordered the holy priest to be set at liberty. A few days afterwards, St. John was crossing the bridge over the river Moldau, which flows through the city of Prague. It was night. The holy confessor noticed that men were following him slowly. He recommended himself to God, and went on courageously. When he had reached the middle of the bridge, just above the most rapid part of the current, the ruffians who were following rushed upon him, bound him hand and foot, and cast him into the river.

146

There was none to witness the sacrilege, but the all-seeing eye of God beheld it. And God soon revealed the murderous deed and proclaimed the sanctity of his servant. A thousand brilliant lights—like twinkling stars—appeared on the dark flood, and floated over the body of the glorious martyr. The people rushed in crowds to behold the wonder. The tyrant himself witnessed it from his palace window. He could murder the glorious confessor, but he could not prevent the people from honoring him. Next morning the priests of the city, with the bishop at their head, followed by vast numbers of people, went in solemn procession and carried the body of the brave martyr in triumph to the cathedral. The church now honors St. John of Nepomuck as a saint and martyr, and his blessed tongue, which refused to violate the seal of confession, is still incorrupt after a lapse of more than three hundred years, and appears as if it still belonged to a living man. Thus suffered and died St. John of Nepomuck, rather than break the seal of confession, and so must every Catholic priest suffer and die rather than breathe a word of what he has heard in confession.

Every priest can say most truthfully with St. Augustine: " That which I know by confession is less known to me than that which I do not know at all." Yes, the breast of the priest, of this angel of peace, is a sealed abyss which neither the fire nor the sword of tyrants can open. The law which shuts the lips of the confidant of our secrets is so rigidly strict that no interest in the world—not even the safety of an empire, not even the safety of his own life, nay, not even the safety of any kind of good imaginable—can authorize its violation.

It may be further observed that if any one forms the habit of concealing faults, venial though they be, he exposes himself to the danger of having, at the hour of death, to withstand the fierce assaults of his hellish foes, who at that last moment avail themselves of every slight advantage, and bring up against him all his sins, mortal and venial, to throw his poor soul into consternation ; and if they chance to find sins not confessed, even though these be not looked upon by us as mortal, they exaggerate and magnify them in their baneful light, and make them appear greater than they really are, in order to force the sinner into discouragement, dejection, and despair of God's mercy. Venerable Bede relates that a certain soldier, who was a great favorite of King Coered, was often exhorted by him to go to confession, as the king was aware of the ungodly life the man was leading, and with how many sins his soul was defiled. But the soldier parried all the pious king's endeavors, by promising to fulfil his duty at some more convenient season. Being at length seized with a dangerous disease, the king, for the love he bore him, went in person to visit him, and profited by the occasion to exhort him anew to settle his accounts with God by an exact confession. The sick man replied that he meant to confess on his recovery, because he feared that if he should confess before getting well, his friends might say that he did it out of fear of death. The king most graciously returned to pay him a second visit, and on his entering the room the sick man began to exclaim: " Sire, what do you want with me now ? You can give me no help !" " What folly is this ?" replied the king, in an indignant tone. " No folly," replied the dying man, " but the very truth. Know thou that but a few minutes ago there came into the room two youths of most engaging appearance, who presented me with a book, beautiful indeed to look at, but very, very small in size. In it I saw the list of my good deeds registered ; but, good God ! how few and how trifling they are ! Behind these youths appeared a group of infernal spirits, horrible to behold, one of whom bore on his shoulders a vast volume of great weight, which contained, written in dread characters, the list of my sins. I read there not only my grievous but even my most trivial offences, those which I committed in passing thought. At the first appearance of this frightful vision, the chief of the infernal crew said to these two angelic youths: 'What are you staying here for, since you have neither part nor lot in this man, who is already our prey?' 'Take him, then,' replied the latter, 'and lead him whither the burden of his iniquities is weighing him down.' At these words they disappeared. Then one demon struck me a blow with a fork on the head, another on the feet, which makes me suffer fearful torments, and I now feel them creeping into my very vitals, whence they will soon tear out my wretched soul."* Having said this, he breathed his last most miserably.

Mark well that the devils reproached this wretched man with the sins he had committed by passing thoughts, although they were well aware that he was laden with a multitude of the most grievous sins, which would have sufficed for his damnation. Certain it is that the enemy has often made use of venial sins at the hour of death as powerful engines of war for the undoing of the servants of God. Ecclesiastical history bears witness to the truth of this statement.

We should, therefore, discover to our confessor all the temptations of the demon, and all our evil inclinations. We should confess with simplicity—that is, without duplicity or excuses, or cloaking our failings. To excuse the evil intent whereby we have sinned is not to confess, but rather to hide and excuse faults. This is not to appease but rather to irritate the Divine Majesty. We should not strive to excuse our sin or give it another face, either alleging that we have been led into it by the persuasion of others, or else by enlarging on the occasions which have tempted us to transgress. Women, especially, are too apt to commit this fault in their confessions. They like to tell long stories, into

* *Hist. Eccl.*, lib. v. c. 14.

which they interweave the history of their sins at full
length ; the upshot of which is that they lay the blame on
their neighbors, or on such of their household, servants or
other people, as may have given occasion to their transgressions. At times, too, it happens that, overcome by a certain shame, they excuse their intention, giving it some color
of goodness, or at least making it appear less bad than it
really was. For God's sake, let them be on their guard
against such double-dealing, as this mode of confessing sins
is excusing rather than accusing themselves of their faults.
In this manner of confessing they run great risk of not receiving pardon at all, or at least of not deriving from the
sacrament all those advantages which they hoped to
receive.

Let every one, then, approach this sacrament with an efficacious sorrow for sin, to which must be joined profound
humility and an unshaken trust in God's mercy. Let all
declare with great simplicity, and without palliation or excuse, all their sins as well as their evil dispositions, such as
generally give rise to sins. By doing this frequently, especially when burdened with some notable transgression, not
only shall we be wholly cleansed, but we shall, moreover,
gain strength against similar falls for the future.

It is true that the fulfilment of the duty of confessing our
sins is difficult, but in complying with this duty we must not
consider the difficulty, but rather our salvation, and the in-
valuable peace that flows therefrom. The confessional is not
a tribunal established to brand the guilty one with disgrace,
nor to pronounce a sentence that may ruin his reputation or
dishonor his memory, but a tribunal whose office it is to re-
establish us in our forfeited birthrights, and to bring back
to our souls that heavenly peace and happiness which had
been banished from it by sin.

See the sinner after confession : his countenance is radiant
with beauty ; his step has become again light and elastic.

because he has thrown off a load that bent him to the earth ; his soul, feeling itself once more free and the companion of angels, reflects upon its features the holy joy with which it is inebriated ; he smiles upon those whom he meets, and every one sees that he is happy. He has again entered that sweet alliance with God, whom he can now justly call his Father ; he trembles now no more when he lifts his eyes to heaven ; he hopes, he loves ; he sees himself reinstated in his dignity of a child of God, and he respects himself. Now that the soul rules over the body, a supernatural strength vivifies and animates him; he feels himself burning with zeal and energy to do good; a new sun has risen upon his life, and everything in him puts on the freshness of youth.

Confession is resurrection—sweet resurrection, indeed. Oh ! what happiness and consoling joy dost thou bring us. Ah ! how unhappy are they who know not the sublimity of confession, who know not the calm and peace that follow from it.

O confession ! precious pledge of the immense love of our Divine Master ! Oh ! the sweet, the delicious tears with which thou bedewest our cheeks ! Oh! the gnawing remorse to which thou puttest an end ! What undefinable happiness, what unspeakable peace dost thou bring to poor sinners ! How many men who live in the lap of ease and affluence, who are clothed in purple and gold, have searched the whole world to find a little peace for their souls, and have only been able to find it in confession !

Fortune, with an unsparing hand, had lavished all her favors upon them, and the world all its honors ; health and strength had been given them ; and still their life was a burden and weighed heavily upon their shoulders. They came to kneel in the confessional, and by revealing what was hidden, what was so heavily pressing upon them, they instantly found that which they looked for in vain through the world—they found the first, the most desirable of all good—ease of mind and peace of conscience. Among the thousands of examples which could be inserted, the pleasing instance of the conversion of a brave officer by a sermon of Father Brydaine will suffice.

Wishing to hear so illustrious a preacher, the officer entered the church at the very moment that this pious priest was speaking on the advantages of a general confession. The officer, convinced of his arguments, immediately formed the resolution of going to confession. Accordingly, he went up to the pulpit, spoke to Father Brydaine, and decided upon remaining there until the end of the retreat. He made his confession with all the sentiments of a true penitent. It seemed to him, as he himself said, that a heavy load was taken off from his head. The day on which he had the happiness of receiving absolution saw him bathed in tears as he left the confessional—in those sweet tears that love and gratitude drew in torrents from his eyes. He followed the saintly father into the sacristy, and there, before a number of other missionaries, the faithful and edifying officer thus expressed the sentiments with which he was animated :

"Gentlemen, I beg you to listen to me, and you especially, Father Brydaine. Never in my life have I felt any pleasure equal to that which I feel since I have made my peace with God. Really I do not believe that Louis XV., whom I have served for thirty-six years, can be happier than I am. No, the king, in all the magnificence that surrounds his throne, though seated in the lap of pleasure, is not so contented and happy as I am since I shook off the horrible load of my sins."

And then throwing himself at Father Brydaine's feet and taking his hands in his, "How I ought to thank God," said he, "for having led me by the hand, as it were, to this place. O father ! nothing was farther from my thoughts than that which you have induced me to do. I can never forget you. I beg of you to pray to God that He may give me time to do penance ; if He assists me I feel that nothing will appear too difficult to me." Such is the joy of every prodigal son of the church after a good confession.

Yes, the confessional is the threshold of the Father's house ; it is at the confessional that the unhappy prodigal finds an indulgent Father, who pardons and embraces him. It is here that the sad tale of woe ever finds an attentive ear, that sorrow is never useless, and that a sigh from the heart of man is always sure to penetrate the heart of God.

It is here that that unheard-of scene between three persons takes place, where the sinner fills the office of accuser, accused, and witness; and the priest that of instructor and judge—and that in the presence of a God who is present only to execute and ratify the sentence. Here everything is divine, everything mysterious. Here justice and mercy unite in the kiss of peace. Here hell is closed for the guilty one, because he has laid open his heart. Here heaven comes down to the sinner, because the sinner humbles himself. Here the fires of God's judgments are quenched in the tears of repentance. Here, by one act of obedience and humility, the proud sinner cancels a whole life of iniquity and rebellion. Here shines again that light which banishes incertitude and remorse, and which establishes anew the interrupted communion of man with God and His saints. Let a man be ever so disfigured with crime, let him be so poor as not to have even a crust of bread, or let him be so rich as not to be able any longer to form an unsatisfied wish ; let him be so unhappy as not even to wish for hope, or so devoured by remorse of conscience as to be unable to enjoy a moment's repose or an instant of forgetfulness ; and then let him come hither and cast himself on his knees, for here there is an ear to listen to him, a power capable of absolving him, and a tender heart still able and willing to love him.

He shall not be required to make known either his name,

153

rank, or position in society ; all that shall be enacted from him is a hearty sorrow for his sins, and an humble obedience to that voice that invites him to be converted and to change his ways. God, who sees and knows all things, requires no more of him. See, already peace comes back to him, and he has gained heaven; pardon descends upon his head, and he who imparts it to him in the name of God knows but this : that he has absolved a sinner, and made him unspeakably happy. Indeed, without confession, without this salutary institution, guilty man would fall into despair. Into what bosom could he discharge the load that weighs so heavily on his heart ? Into his friend's ? Ah ! who can trust in the friendship of men ! Would he make the trackless deserts his confidants ? To the guilty one the very deserts seem to re-echo continually to the loud cries of his conscience. When nature and men are merciless, it is a touching thing to find a God ready to pardon. The Catholic religion alone is the first and only one that has joined together, like two sisters, innocence and repentance.

Saint Mary Magdalen

CHAPTER VIII.

THE PRODIGAL'S SORROW—CONTRITION.

MORE than eighteen centuries have passed since the Son of God accomplished the great work of redemption by His bitter passion and death. As the time of His sufferings drew nigh, Jesus entered Jerusalem with His disciples ; and the people of the city, on learning of His approach, hastened forth to meet Him. In their hands they bore branches of the palm and the olive ; they spread their garments on the ground before Jesus ; they filled the air with loud hosannas, and with sweet hymns of praise and gladness. But strange to say, amidst the music and rejoicing—amidst the glory of His triumphant entry, Jesus is sad ; Jesus weeps and sobs aloud as if His heart would break. This is indeed strange beyond expression. Was Jesus sad because He disliked rejoicings ? Oh ! no. For we see Him often present at banquets of the Pharisees. We see Him present at the merry wedding feast of Cana, where, in order to increase the gaiety, He works an unheard-of miracle, and changes water into wine. Jesus was no enemy of innocent rejoicings. Why, then, does He weep midst the rejoicings of His triumphant entry into Jerusalem ? Jesus Himself tells us the cause of His tears. He protests that He weeps because Jerusalem does not know Him. " O Jerusalem, didst thou but know, this day, the things that are for thy peace ; but now they are hidden from thine eyes." * What can this mean ? Why, the whole city can scarce contain itself for joy. No sound is heard save that of praise and gladness.

* Luke xix.

"Blessed be the king who cometh in the name of the Lord, peace in heaven, and glory on high." * Such is the triumphant hymn with which the people greet Jesus ; and yet Jesus weeps and laments because the city does not know Him. "Oh ! didst thou but know and understand this day."

Such was the welcome which Jesus received from the Jewish people ; such, too, is the welcome which He receives at the present day from so many of His own Christian people. He is welcomed by all, He is known but to few. Like the Jewish people, many Christians welcome Jesus ; they hasten to the sacraments with every outward mark of devotion ; but like the Jews, too, though they welcome Jesus, though they receive Jesus, they do not know or care to know Jesus. In spite of the solemnity of the season, in spite of the outward marks of devotion, so many Christians of the present day often approach the sacraments with such little preparation, with such unworthy dispositions, that instead of being a joy and honor to Jesus, they rather fill His heart with sadness. They load Him with insult.

Let us return to Jerusalem a few days after the triumphant entry of Jesus. Behold this very same Jewish people. They are following an unhappy criminal who is being led to death. Ask them who this criminal is, and they will tell you, "It is Jesus of Nazareth." What ! Jesus of Nazareth ? Is it possible ? Is not this the same Jesus who was welcomed only a few days ago with such unparalleled honors ? Is not this the same people who but a few days ago cried out, "Blessed is he that cometh in the name of the Lord"; and now their hoarse cry rings wildly through the air, "Crucify him ! crucify him !" Yes, it is the very same Jesus ; it is the very same people. No wonder, then, that Jesus wept on the day of His triumph. No wonder

* Luke xix.

that He complained that this people did not know Him. O ungrateful people ! could you not dishonor Jesus by a shameful death, without first honoring Him with such a glorious triumph ?

But let us turn to ourselves. Were a stranger to pass through the city at the season of Lent, were he to see the churches so well filled, and the confessionals so well crowded with penitents, what a good opinion would he form of the Catholics here. Wherever we turn we behold eyes filled with tears, countenances stamped with contrition—every· where signs of sincere devotion. Here truly, he would say, Jesus is honored; here He rejoices, here He celebrates a glorious triumph. Yes; but return here in two months, in two weeks even, and the penitent faces will be seen at parties, balls, theatres, frolics, in drinking-saloons; at the gambling-table the very same hands; in families, among relatives and neighbors, the very same quarrels; in the stores the same false weights, the same fraud ; the old curses and blasphemies will be heard in the streets and public places. This is indeed a change of scene, and this change of scene is renewed every Easter.

Whence comes this fickleness ? The Jewish people, in the impulse of the moment, hastened forth to meet Jesus without well knowing whom they welcomed. So in like manner many Christians, carried away by the devotion of the season, hasten to welcome Jesus without knowing Him ; they hasten to be reconciled to Jesus without understanding well whom it is they have offended. The prophet bitterly bewails such blindness : " There is not one who does penance for his sins, not one who asks himself seriously, What have I done ? " * This is the origin of the sad inconstancy of the greater part of Christians. Did they, like the Prodigal, but fully understand the greatness of their sins, they would, like him, truly repent of them. But such is not the case

* Jer. viii.

They have no true contrition, and, consequently, they soor. fall again and again into the very same sins that they have but a short time before confessed.

Now, it is of faith that true sorrow for our sins is absolutely necessary for salvation, for if there is no true sorrow there can be no pardon. The examen of conscience is necessary; but were we to spend a whole year in examining our conscience without sincere sorrow or contrition, we cannot obtain pardon.

Confession is necessary; but it may happen that we forget a sin, or cannot find a confessor, or that we cannot speak the language of the priest, or that we have lost our speech. In such cases it will be sufficient if we make an act of perfect contrition, with the sincere resolution to confess our sins as soon as possible. But were we to confess all our sins with even the minutest accompanying circumstances, if we have no contrition we cannot obtain pardon.

Satisfaction is necessary; but it is sometimes impossible, and may be dispensed with. A person, for instance, may be too poor to make restitution; in that case it will suffice if he have the sincere desire to restore as soon as possible. But though he were to restore everything and had not true sorrow, he could not receive forgiveness.

Absolution is necessary; but sometimes there is no priest at hand. It will be sufficient then to make an act of perfect contrition, and have the sincere desire to confess as soon as possible, and we shall be forgiven; but were we to be absolved by all the bishops and priests of the Church, even by the Pope himself, and had not true sorrow, we should not receive forgiveness.

So important, so necessary is contrition that, though a sinner were guilty of all the crimes that ever have been or ever will be committed on the face of the earth—if he has but true contrition, he can and ought to be absolved ; while, on the contrary, he who has only committed a slight venial sin—if he has no contrition, cannot and should not receive absolution.

God will not pardon without contrition. " It is," as Tertullian says, " the only price for which God pardons." God cannot pardon without contrition, for to be without sorrow for an offence is to give new and continued offence.

True contrition, then, is absolutely necessary. To have the desire for contrition is good; but the wish is not sufficient. Tears are good, but tears are not sufficient. It is not sufficient to look sad and strike the breast again and again ; it is not sufficient to read the act of contrition out of a book ; it is not sufficient to mutter the act of contrition with the lips. No ! contrition must be real and heartfelt.

What then is contrition ? Contrition is a hearty sorrow for having offended God. It includes a sincere hatred of sin, and the firm resolution to offend God no more. Every sin and vice, as our dear Saviour Himself declares, proceeds from the heart and has its seat in the heart. When we sin, it is, properly speaking, not our eyes, or ears, or tongue, the members of our body that sin, but the soul, animating our members. The soul uses the senses as the instruments of sin. It is the soul, the will, that sins, and consequently it is the soul, the will, that must repent. Our contrition, then must necessarily be interior and heartfelt. The very word contrition itself implies its true nature. Contrition is derived from the Latin word " conterere," which means to bruise, to crush, to break. To have true, heartfelt contrition, therefore, means to be heartbroken for having offended our dear Lord.

Tears are not necessary as expressions of sorrow for sin :

the feeling of pain is not necessary; and yet the sorrow must be real and earnest, proceeding from the heart. Now, if sincere, heartfelt contrition is so necessary, what are we to think of those penitents who approach the confessional and confess their sins with such cool indifference, that one might be tempted to suppose they had come for no other purpose than to relate some interesting anecdote ? If the priest tells them to make an act of contrition, he must often observe, to his grief, that they do not know how to make the act. Many of them do not even know what contrition, true sorrow, is, or what it has to do with confession. The greater part, however, know, indeed, how to make an act of contrition, but unfortunately, even their contrition consists generally in striking the breast a few times, and in muttering a certain formula of prayer which they learned in their childhood. If the priest asks such a penitent whether he is sorry for his sins, the answer is of course " yes " ; but it is a " yes " that evidently does not come from the heart—it is a " yes " that is just about equivalent to " no."

It is not the number and enormity of the sins that fill the priest with pain and anxiety. It is the want of disposition, of true contrition, in the penitent, that causes him often the most cruel martyrdom.

The sorrow for sin must not only be sincere and heartfelt —it must also be a sorrow above every other sorrow. The sorrow which we feel at the loss of an object is proportionate to the value of the object. But God is a good infinitely superior to every other possible good. Consequently the loss of God should cause us greater sorrow than the loss of every other good. Great is the sorrow of a poor orphan as she stands by the death-bed of her beloved mother—as she gazes on her pale, cold brow, and on those loving eyes which shall open upon her never more. Yet our sorrow for having lost God by sin must be far greater. Great is the sorrow of a tender mother as she bends over the lifeless

161

body of her only child, the child of her hope and love. And yet our sorrow for having offended God must exceed even this sorrow. Yes, if we are truly sorry for our sins, we must be willing to lose our health, our riches, and our honor; to lose friends and parents, to endure every pain, and even death itself, rather than lose God by consenting to another mortal sin. It is not necessary that this sorrow for losing God should be sensibly felt. We may indeed experience more sorrow at the loss of our honor—at the loss of a dear friend or relative ; nevertheless we must be ready to lose all rather than lose God. We may feel more terror at the sight of torment and death, and yet we must be ready to suffer the most cruel death rather than consent to a single mortal sin.

Contrition must not only be interior and sovereign, it must also be supernatural. We must be sorry for having sinned, because by sin we have offended and lost so good a God.

Antiochus Epiphanes, King of Syria, committed many enormous crimes. He ordered the faithful Jews to be cruelly massacred; he plundered the Temple, and desecrated the Holy of Holies. But the vengeance of God was swift and terrible. The impious king was stricken down with an incurable disease. A most excruciating pain tortured him; his body was devoured by worms ; his rotten flesh fell piecemeal from his body, and the stench which proceeded from him was intolerable. The unhappy tyrant began now to repent of his crimes. He promised God that he would restore everything he had stolen from the Temple ; he even promised that he would renounce infidelity, travel all over the world, and preach everywhere the true God. This looked like an extraordinary contrition ; yet the Holy Ghost tells us of this man in holy Scripture : "This wicked man prayed to God, but in vain ! He received no mercy !*

* 2 Mach. iii. 13.

He died in a strange land, miserably in his sins. And why so ? Is not God infinitely merciful ? Has not God sworn by Himself that " He wills not the death of the sinner, but that he be converted and live ? " Why then did not God pardon this sinner ? Although this wicked man wept bitter tears, though he promised to restore everything, though he promised to change his wicked life—he, nevertheless, received no pardon, because his sorrow was only natural sorrow. He did not weep for having offended God. He only wept because he suffered such cruel torments, and because he saw that he was soon to die. His contrition was not supernatural. Look at many a drunkard : he weeps ; he curses the hour in which he first tasted liquor. But why does he weep ? Is it because he has offended God ? Oh ! no. He weeps because he has lost his situation—because he has fallen into disgrace. His sorrow is therefore only natural. He cannot receive pardon on that account.

The swindler and the thief are sorry for what they have done. But is it because they have offended God ? No ! They are sorry because they have been arrested and put in prison. Such sorrow is vain before God, and can merit no pardon.

The unhappy young man who has wasted his health and happiness in striving to satisfy a brutal passion, laments and curses the day on which he was first led into sin. But does he weep for having offended God ? No; he weeps because he has ruined his health, because he finds himself branded with a shameful disease, because he feels that he is a burden to himself, an outcast, an object of scorn to his fellow-men. His contrition is, therefore, not supernatural, and cannot merit pardon.

The unfortunate who sighs and weeps like another repentant Magdalen, weeps not because she has offended God, but because she has lost her honor ; because she must now hide her face behind the veil of shame. Her sorrow is there-**fore only natural sorrow; she can receive no pardon for it.**

Contrition, then, in order to be acceptable to God, must be supernatural. It must come from God. We must be sorry for our sins because by them we have offended so good a God, and thereby lost heaven and deserved hell.

But contrition must not only be interior, sovereign, and supernatural, it must also be universal. We must be sorry for every sin, every mortal sin, without exception. King Saul was commanded by God to destroy all the wicked inhabitants of Amelec, and not to spare even a single one. Saul obeyed, but his obedience was not perfect. He destroyed everything, he burned down everything, he killed all the common people, but the king, who was the most wicked of all, he spared. God punished Saul for this want of obedience by taking away his crown and his life. There are many Catholics who, when they go to confession, act just as Saul acted. God has commanded them, under pain of eternal damnation, to destroy every mortal sin, and every affection for mortal sin, by a sincere and universal contrition. They obey, indeed, but their obedience is not perfect. By contrition they destroy the slight, every-day failings ; but there is one pet sin that they always spare, one wicked passion, their ruling passion, which they do not destroy by a true and earnest contrition. A certain person, for instance, comes to confession. He confesses that he cursed, that he was angry. He is perhaps truly sorry for these sins ; but he has also been drunk several times, and for this sin, though he may confess it, he has no real, earnest sorrow. Such a man's confession is a sacrilege ; his sins are not forgiven.

Here is another sinner. He confesses that he has eaten meat a few times on Friday, that he has missed Mass and worked a few times on Sunday, but he has also eaten meat without necessity on fast-days, he has also missed Mass and worked on holydays of obligation without necessity. These sins he hardly remembers, and has no real contrition for them.   He has no sorrow for all his mortal sins, and, there-fore, he can receive pardon for none.   His confession is worthless.

Another confesses that he has stolen and cheated very much; that he has wantonly damaged his neighbor's property.   He is sorry for these sins, he is even willing to make restitution to the best of his power.   But there is another sin for which he has no real, earnest sorrow.   He often takes pleasure in immodest thoughts and desires ; he is a slave to the accursed habit of self-abuse.   For these sins he is not truly sorry.   His confession is, therefore, a mockery; he can receive no pardon from God.

The mother of a family confesses all her sins, and is truly sorry for them.   But there are some sins that she scarcely ever mentions in confession, some sins for which she has no true contrition.   She allows her children to remain out late at night ; she does not keep them away from dangerous company—from balls and parties; she allows them to read sentimental and immoral books—novels, trashy love poetry, and the like.   Under the veil of marriage, she commits un natural sins ; she tries to hinder the most sacred laws of nature.   Her sins are not forgiven.

A young girl confesses that she has been proud and vain, that she has been disobedient to her parents a few times She is perhaps sorry for these sins.   But there is another sin which she does not mention in confession, and for which she has no true sorrow.   She often reads sentimental and dangerous books ; she often remains out late at night ; she keeps dangerous company; she sometimes allows improper liberties ; she often harbors wicked thoughts and desires These sins she does not confess, and, even if she confesses them, she has no true sorrow for them.   Such a person's confession is worthless ; it is a sacrilege.   She does not obtain pardon from God ; but the curse of God weighs on her soul; and until she truly repents of these sins, no

165

priest in Christendom, no bishop, no pope, can absolve her.

We must not only confess all our mortal sins, but we must also be truly sorry for them, otherwise we can obtain pardon for none. The reason for this is, that God never has pardoned, and by an unchangeable decree has bound Himself never to pardon, any one unless he first repents of all his sins, and repents of them from motives of a supernatural character.

Again, sorrow for our sins, to be good, must be accompanied by a firm resolve not to fall again into the same sins. To repent truly and sincerely is to grieve over the evil we have done, and to refrain from doing again the evil over which we grieve. In order that our past sins may not be imputed to us, sorrow and tears are not enough, amendment is also necessary.

Cesarius relates * a frightful occurrence which took place at Paris. There was in Paris a canon of the Church of Notre Dame, who was a priest in name, but certainly not in the practice of the virtues becoming his holy state. This canon, being at the point of death, entered into himself, acknowledged the wretched state of his soul, and seemed to be a really penitent and entirely changed man. Having sent for his confessor, he accused himself, with abundant tears, of all his sins, and received the holy viaticum and extreme unction with every outward token of piety. He then gently breathed out his soul in peace. After his death a magnificent burial service was prepared, and the day appointed for it was so fine that it looked as if heaven and earth were leagued together in order to enhance the pomp of the funeral obsequies. Every one deemed him the happiest man that had ever appeared on the face of the earth, since, after having enjoyed this world to the full, he had by so happy a death secured for himself the glory of

* *Mirac.*, lib. ii. c. 15.

Paradise. Such was the common talk ; for man sees what is outside, but God beholds what lies hidden within. After a few days the canon appeared to a servant of God, and brought him the sad news that he was damned. "But how so ?" asked the holy man, quite astounded ; "you confessed with sorrow and tears, and received the holy sacraments with devotion." "True," said the lost soul, "I did confess, and I was sorry, yet not with an efficacious sorrow, since my will, in the very act of repenting, felt itself spurred on to sin afresh ; and I thought it quite impossible that, if restored to health, I should not return to that which I so dearly loved. So that while I detested the evil I had committed, I had no earnest and firm purpose of renouncing it." Having said this, he disappeared.

Sorrow for our sins, moreover, must be accompanied by sincere humility. "God will never despise a contrite heart when he sees that it is humbled."* The publican in the Gospel looked upon himself as one of the greatest sinners in the world. He durst not so much as lift up his eyes to heaven, but held them downcast, and with shame on his countenance fixed them on the ground. He smote his breast, and thus moved God to compassion, appeased his wrath, and obtained his pardon. Such are the sentiments with which we should approach the holy tribunal of penance. For the inward shame which we feel at the sight of our offences has a large share in obtaining our pardon; and it is out of mercy to us that God has decreed that, in order to obtain forgiveness, it should not be enough to repent in secret and be seen by Him alone, but that we must express our sorrow at the feet of the priest, and thus be covered with that most wholesome confusion which is of so great avail to obtain pardon for our sins.

If, like the Prodigal, we sincerely acknowledge before God the evil we have done in sinning, if we consider the

* Psalm l.

greatness of the God whom we have offended, if we consider our own vileness and audacity in daring to insult a God of so great a majesty, we shall naturally feel humbled and shall appear like criminals before the Lord, own our abjection with great confusion, detest our misdeeds, and implore forgiveness: "Father, I have sinned against heaven and before thee, I am not now worthy to be called thy son; make me as one of thy hired servants." *

The sinner thus humbled before God presents so touching an object in his sight that He is instantly roused to compassionate pity, forgives the transgressions of the culprit, and hastens in all tenderness to clasp him lovingly to his bosom, to treat him not as a criminal, nor as one who has ever been guilty, but as a beloved child. With such humble contrition, with sorrowful confusion, should the sinner draw nigh to the laver of confession. He may then rest assured that our loving Redeemer, beholding him in these good dispositions, will not fail to shower down His most precious blood in such abundance on him as to cleanse him from all stain and render him whiter and purer than the lily.

But let it be observed that this humility, which should ever accompany sorrow for sin, must not be false. Humility is false whenever it is not joined with a strong and firm hope of obtaining forgiveness. There are two sorts of humility: one is the gift of God, the other comes from the devil. The humility which is God's gift brings with it, indeed, a knowledge of our sins and miseries, but has this property, that, while it lowers the soul in its own estimation, it raises it to hope, and finally leaves it all calm and reposing in the arms of the Divine goodness. The humility, however, which is counterfeit, and from the devil, brings with it, in like manner, a knowledge of our own sins and weakness, but it has this most injurious quality, that, while it bends low the soul, it takes away hope, or at least dimin-

* Luke xv. 18, 19.

168

ishes it, and leaves us full of cowardice, diffidence, and discouragement. The humility which is God's gift is holy; that which comes from the devil is wicked. The humility which comes from God disposes us for pardon, whilst the humility that comes from the devil prevents forgiveness. Our confessions, therefore, must be made in a spirit of faith and hope ; they should be accompanied with a sorrow not only humble, but full of faith and trust in God. Without such hope we should never obtain pardon, were we to seek it for all eternity; because sorrow for sin, unaccompanied by hope of forgiveness, so far from appeasing, only irritates Divine mercy. Cain repented of his crime after he had murdered his own brother; but because he did not trust in the Divine goodness, his sorrow availed him nothing. "My iniquity," he said in his folly, "is greater than may deserve pardon." * Judas Iscariot in like manner repented, and exclaimed, with tears flowing down his cheeks, "I have sinned in betraying innocent blood." † And further, he made restitution of the money for which he had bartered away the precious life of his divine Master. But what did all this avail him ? Nothing whatever. His sorrow was devoid of any gleam of hope ; and, giving himself up for lost, he went and hanged himself on a tree.

Of such a nature is the repentance of certain persons who, after falling into some serious faults, or seeing that they relapse constantly into the same sins, are filled with bitterness, distrust, and false humility, and say to themselves : "God will not pardon me; I think He has turned His back upon me, for my weakness is beyond endurance, and I am continually yielding to the same faults." Now, this is the contrition of Judas and Cain, devoid of all trust in God's goodness.

The devil appeared once to Faverius, a disciple of St. Bruno, while he was dangerously ill on his sick bed, and,

* Gen. iv. 13   † Matt. xxvii. 4.

after terrifying him in many ways, began to remind him of his sins, and to throw them in his face with impudent assurance. The servant of God replied that he had already confessed these sins and received absolution, and therefore had every cause to trust that God had pardoned him. "Confessed your sins! Confessed your sins!" replied the fiend. "You have not told all; you have not made a proper confession; you have not explained the circumstances of your sins. Your confessions are all invalid; they are good for nothing; they will serve only to make your judgment the heavier." The holy monk, thus reminded of his faults, shown to him by the fiend in that accursed light which makes us see things in a false medium, and represents God as always using fire and the knife in His treatment of sick souls, was greatly alarmed, and began to be tortured by the most agonizing scruples, being so horror-stricken and full of dismay that he was on the point of falling headlong into the abyss of despair. But the ever Blessed Virgin, the true Mother of mercy, who never forsakes those who are really devoted to her, appeared to him most opportunely at this terrible moment, with her Divine Infant in her arms, and addressed him as follows: "What fearest thou, Faverius? wherefore lose heart? Hope and be of good cheer; thou hast all but reached the port. All thy sins have been forgiven thee by my most winning Child. Of this I give thee my assurance." * At these words the racking and anguish felt by the dying man at the thoughts of his sins gave place to a humble, confiding, peaceful sorrow, and shortly after he breathed his last in great calm of soul. From this we may perceive the difference between contrition, which is God's gift, and that which comes from the devil. This latter is a sorrow full of diffidence and disquiet; the former is a trusting and peaceful repentance. Let every one, then, ever strive after the gift of

Ex Annal. Carthus.

God, and take care to possess it whenever he goes to cor fession. This kind of sorrow alone appeases God, obtains pardon for sin, and perfectly reconciles the soul with God.

There are many persons who seem to think that the whole efficacy of the sacrament of penance depends on lengthy details, and in saying in many words what could be all said in very few. The sign of a good confession is not the multitude of words, but the sorrow of the heart, and him alone may we judge to be converted, and to have made a good confession, who strives to blot out by heartfelt sorrow those sins of which his tongue makes the outward avowal. The verbal confession of sin is to be valued only inasmuch as it is the expression of a true and heartfelt repentance. Our dear Lord cursed the barren fig-tree. which, though full of branches and leaves, yet bore no fruit; so does He reject and abhor such confessions as abound in many unnecessary words, but are barren of the fruit of efficacious contrition. Sorrow, and great sorrow, is what is needed, not long explanations and needless details, if confession is to restore the sinner to grace. The truth of this is confirmed by the following incident.

Cæsarius Heisterbach relates that a young student at Paris, having fallen into many very grievous sins, betook himself to the monastery of St. Victor, and, calling the prior, fell at his feet in order to accuse himself of them. Scarce had he began to open his lips when his contrition became so vehement that his utterance was checked, and his confession hindered, by tears, groans, and convulsive sobs. The confessor, seeing that the youth was unable from excessive grief to say another word, bade him write down his sins on a sheet of paper, and come back again when he had done so, hoping that by this means the young man would find it easier to make a confession of all his crimes. He complied, and returned to the same priest; but no sooner did he begin to read from· his paper than, overcome anew with sorrow

171

and tears, he was unable to proceed. The confessor then asked him for the paper, and as in reading it a doubt arose in his mind on some point, he begged the penitent's leave to show his confession to the abbot, in order to get his opinion. The contrite youth willingly consented, and forthwith the prior went to see the abbot and put the paper into his hands. The abbot on opening it found nothing but a blank sheet, without so much as a single stroke of the pen upon the page. "How now," said he, "do you want me to read what is not written ? " " But," replied the prior, " I have this moment read on that very paper the full confession of this my penitent." Then both began to examine the paper afresh, and found that the sins had been blotted out of it, even as they were already blotted out of the conscience of the sorrowing youth.* Behold ! this young student had not yet made his confession, and still had already received a full pardon ; for though he had said nothing with his tongue, he had spoken much with his heart, and nothing now remained for him to do save to fulfil the obligation of subjecting his sins to the sacramental absolution.

One day a great sinner went to hear a sermon by St. Antony of Padua. Immediately after the sermon the sinner approached the saint, and entreated him to hear his confession. Though greatly fatigued, Antony immediately entered his confessional to console the heart of the penitent. But the latter was so overcome with sorrow as to be quite unable to make his confession, his sobs and groans completely depriving him of the power of speech. As the saint was greatly pressed for time, he told his penitent to go home and write down his sins and then come back. The man obeyed : he went home, wrote down his confession, and then returned to his confessor. Now, when St. Antony opened the paper, he saw with joy that he held in his hand a blank sheet of such dazzling whiteness that no one would

* *Histor. Mirac.*, lib. v. cap. 10.

ever suppose it had been written upon. The saint looked upon this prodigy as the happy indication of perfect contrition.

The grace of true and sincere sorrow for our sins is no water of this earth, but of heaven. "If any assert," says the Council of Trent, "that without a preceding inspiration and grace of the Holy Ghost man can believe, hope, and love, or repent, in such a manner as he ought, let him be anathema." "No one," says the holy Church, "can repent of his sins in such a manner as he ought without a particular grace of God."

Man, it is true, can of himself commit sin and offend God grievously, but to rise again from his fall by heartfelt sorrow he cannot, except by God's grace. Now, this exceedingly great grace will be given to us so much the sooner the more earnestly we pray for it, especially while assisting at the holy sacrifice of the Mass. It was through the blood of Jesus Christ, visibly shed on the cross, that the dying malefactor obtained the grace of conversion, of sincere repentance. In like manner, it is through the same blood, invisibly shed at Mass, that the heavenly Father will grant us the grace of true contrition for our sins if we offer to Him the blood of His beloved Son, Jesus Christ, in satisfaction for them, and beseech Him, by the merits of this blood, to have mercy on us.

But as our prayer may not be fervent enough soon to obtain for us this great grace of contrition, let us have recourse to the all-powerful prayer of the Blessed Virgin Mary. She is the refuge of all poor sinners, and she has obtained this unspeakably great favor for the most abandoned sinners, even in their last hour.

St. Teresa gives an account of a merchant who lived at Valladolid. in Spain. He did not live as a good Christian should live ; however, he had some devotion to the Blessed Virgin. When St. Teresa came to the town where the merchant was living, she wanted to find a house for her nuns. The merchant heard that the saint was seeking a house ; so he went to her, and offered to give her a house which belonged to him. He said he would give her the house in honor of the Blessed Virgin Mary. St. Teresa thanked him, and took the house. Two months after this the gentleman suddenly became very ill. He was not able to speak or make a confession. However, he showed by signs that he wished to beg pardon of our Lord for his sins, and soon after died. "After his death," St. Teresa says, "I saw our Lord. He told me that this gentleman had been very near losing his soul ; but He had mercy on him when he was dying, on account of the service he did to His blessed Mother by giving the house in her honor." "I was glad," says St. Teresa, "that his soul was saved, for I was very much afraid it would have been lost on account of his bad life." Our Lord told St. Teresa to get the house finished as soon as possible, because that soul was suffering great torments in Purgatory. It would not come out of Purgatory till the convent was finished and the first Mass said there. When the first Mass was said, St. Teresa went to the rails of the altar to receive Holy Communion. At the moment she knelt down she saw the gentleman standing by the side of the priest. His face was shining with light and joy, and his hands were joined together. He thanked St. Teresa very much for getting his soul out of the fire of Purgatory, and the saint then saw him go up into heaven.

Let us, then, pray ; and let us pray to the Mother of God for contrition, and we shall infallibly obtain this grace through her all-powerful intercession ; for her divine Son, Jesus Christ, can refuse nothing to his Mother.

CHAPTER IX.

WHAT INCREASED THE PRODIGAL'S SORROW — GENERAL CONFESSION.

ONE day the Countess de Joigny sent for St. Vincent de Paul to prepare one of her servants for death. The saint went immediately. His great charity induced the sick man to make a general confession. And, indeed, nothing but a general confession could have saved the dying man ; for he publicly declared that he had never confessed certain mortal sins. The sincerity with which he declared his secret miseries was followed by an inexpressible consolation. The sinner felt that an enormous weight. which had for many years oppressed him, was at length taken off. The most remarkable circumstance was that he passed from one extreme to another. During the three days of life that were still left him, he made several public confessions of the faults which a false shame had always prevented him from confessing hitherto. "Ah ! madam," he exclaimed on beholding the countess enter his room, "I should have been damned on account of several mortal sins which I always concealed in confession ; but Father Vincent has, by his charity, induced me to make all my confessions over again. I am very grateful to Father Vincent, and to you for having sent him to me to prepare me for a happy death." Upon hearing this unexpected confession of her servant, the countess exclaimed: "Alas ! Father Vincent, what must I hear ? How great is my surprise ! What happened to this servant of mine happens, no doubt, to many other people. If this man, who was considered a pious Christian by every one who knew him, could live so long in the state of mortal sin, how great must be the spiritual misery of those whose life is much looser! Alas! my dear father, how many souls are lost! What is to be done? What remedy must be applied to prevent the ruin of so many souls?"

"Ah!" exclaimed St. Vincent, "false shame prevents a great many persons from confessing all their grievous sins. This is the reason why they live constantly in a state of damnation. O my God! how important is it often to inculcate the necessity of a general confession. Persons who have concealed grievous sins in their confession have no other remedy left to recover the grace of God. This farmer himself avowed publicly that he would have been damned had it not been for his general confession. A soul, penetrated with the spirit of true repentance, is filled with so great a hatred for sin that she is ready to confess her sins, not only to the priest, but to every one else whom she meets. I have met with persons who, after a good general confession, wished to make known their sins to the whole world, and I had the greatest difficulty to prevent them from doing so. Although I had strictly forbidden them not to speak to any one of their crimes, yet some would tell me : 'No, father, I will not be silent; I will tell the people how great a sinner I am ; I am the most wicked man in the world; I deserve death.' See, then, what the grace of God can do; see the great sorrow it can produce in the soul! This was the way in which the greatest saints acted. Witness St. Augustine, who made a public confession of his sins in a book which he wrote to that effect ; witness also the great Apostle St. Paul, who tells us, in his Epistles, what sins he committed against God and the Church. These saints made this public confession of their sins in order to make known to the whole world the great mercy which God had exercised in their regard. The grace of God has also produced a similar effect in the soul of this farmer. O my God! how important is it to inculcate the necessity of general confession." *

To many persons a general confession is absolutely necessary for salvation. It is necessary, 1st, to all those who, in any of their former confessions, have wilfully concealed a mortal sin; 2. To those who have confessed their sins without sorrow and a firm purpose of amendment.

But who are those that confess without true sorrow for their sins? They are—

1. All who do not intend to keep the promise to avoid mortal sin which they made in confession.

2. All who are not willing to forgive their enemies.

3. All who have no intention to restore ill-gotten goods, or the good name of their neighbor after having taken it away by slander or detraction.

4. All who are not fully determined to keep away from taverns, grog-shops, and such places as have always proved occasions of sin to them; and

5. All who do not break off sinful company.

Now, the reason why these persons must make a general confession is because their confessions were bad; instead of obtaining forgiveness by them, they only increase their guilt before God. In order to be forgiven they must, 1, confess over again all those mortal sins which they have committed from the time they began to make bad confessions; 2. They must tell in confession how many times they received the sacraments unworthily; and, 3. They must be very sorry for all those sins, and firmly resolve never to commit them again.

There are, however, others to whom a general confession would be hurtful. There are certain scrupulous souls who have already made a general confession, who have confessed even more than was necessary, and yet they cannot

* **Abelly**, *Vie de St. Vincent de Paul.*

177

rest. They wish to be always employed in making general confessions, with the hope of thus removing their fears and troubles. But what is the result ? Their perplexities are always increased, because new apprehensions and scruples of having omitted or of not having sufficiently explained their sins, are continually excited in their minds. Hence, the more they repeat confessions, the more they are stirring up, as it were, a hornet's nest—being stung more than ever with thousands of scruples, and wounded all over with fears and troubles of spirit. The reason of this is that the alarms and terrors which agitate these scrupulous souls are grounded, not on solid reasons, but on baseless apprehensions, which the remembrance of past sins can serve only to encourage and to quicken, so as to double the disturbance in the mind.

But a person may say : " If the sin be really a mortal sin, and if I have not confessed it, shall I be saved ? " " Yes, you will be saved," says St. Alphonsus, St. Thomas Aquinas, and all divines ; " for if, after a careful examination of conscience, a mortal sin has not been told through forgetfulness, it is indirectly forgiven by the sacramental absolution ; because when God forgives one mortal sin, He at the same time forgives all others of which the soul may be guilty."

He who makes as good a confession of his sins as he can obtains, by the sacrament of penance, the forgiveness not only of those sins which he confesses, but also of those which, through forgetfulness, he does not confess. In spite of this failing of the memory, the penitent is in God's grace and in the path of salvation. He should therefore be at peace and never more mention his past sins. He should understand that a general confession is useful for a certain class of persons, but very dangerous and injurious to a person that is always agitated by scruples ; for the repetition of past sins may be productive of grievous detriment to such a soul, and may drive her to despair. Hence good confessors do not permit scrupulous persons to speak of past sins. The remedy for them is not to explain their doubts, but to be silent and obey, believing for certain that God will never ask of them an account of what they have done in obedience to their confessors.

Lastly, there are persons for whom a general confession is most useful ; for those who never made a general confession at all. A general confession gives our confessor a better knowledge of the state of our conscience, of the virtues in which we stand most in need, and of the passions and vices to which we are most inclined ; and he is thus better able to apply proper remedies and give good advice.

A general confession also contributes greatly to humble our soul, to increase the sorrow we feel for our ingratitude towards God, and to make us adopt holy resolutions for the future.

Whilst the prodigal was feeding the swine, he could not help reflecting on the happiness of his brother, and even of his father's servants. He compared his life of degradation with the life he might have enjoyed had he stayed with his father. The grief which he had caused to his father, his ingratitude towards him, his bodily and spiritual misery— all the crimes of his life were before his mind. He could no longer endure this horrible prospect nor the bitter remorse of his conscience. He hastened to make a public confession to his father of all his crimes, with tears in his eyes saying : " Make me as one of thy hired servants."

We too, on looking back at all the faults into which we have fallen during our whole life, cannot fail to be stirred up to a more lively contrition than can be excited by the recollection of those ordinary failings which usually form the matter of the confessions which are called " particular " as distinct from general confessions. Far different, indeed, is the confession and humility which fills the mind at the sight of a whole legion of sins from that which is occasioned by the consciousness of some single fault into which we have but recently been betrayed. One or two regiments cannot have that power against the enemy which is possessed by the vast, serried mass of the battalions of an army. So the one or two faults of which we accuse ourselves in our ordinary confessions cannot have the force which the whole host of our failings possesses to subdue our hearts, to soften them into perfect contrition, and to bring them to a deep sense of humility and inward self-abasement.

This truth of the Catholic faith is wondrously illustrated by what may be read in the fourth step of the well-known *Ladder of Perfection*, by St. John Climacus. A most abandoned youth, touched by the grace of God, and sincerely repenting of his disorderly life, went to one of the monasteries most famous for the holiness of its inmates, and, falling at the feet of the superior, asked permission to be admitted into the community, in order to do penance for his sins. The young man was received. He declared himself ready to make a public confession of his sins in presence of all the monks of the monastery. The following Sunday the monks, two hundred and thirty in number, were gathered together in church. The abbot brought in the young man, who was visibly touched with the deepest compunction. Prostrate in the church, the penitent began, with a flood of tears, to make public confession of all his crimes, distinguishing both their number and kind. Whilst he went on accusing himself of all the murders he had committed, of his many robberies, and repeated sacrileges, the monks were wondrously edified at the sight of a penitence so rarely witnessed. Meanwhile a holy monk saw some one, of majestic and awful appearance, standing with a large roll and a bottle of ink in one hand, and in the other hand a pen. He observed, too, that as each sin was confessed the man crossed it out with his pen ; so that, when the confession was ended, all the sins were cancelled from the paper and from the soul of the young man at the same time.

Now, what was thus visibly shown in the case of that repentant youth happens, in an invisible manner, to all who make a good general confession. All their sins are blotted out at once from the book in which our life is written by God, and from the book of our soul, which then regains its former unsullied purity. In the little book *Triumph of the Blessed Sacrament over Beelzebub ; or, History of Nicola Aubry,* who was possessed by Beelzebub and several other evil spirits, we read the following ·

One day, during one of the exorcisms in church, the evil spirit was chattering and uttering all kinds of nonsense. Suddenly he stopped short and gazed fixedly at a young man who was eagerly forcing his way through the crowd in order to have a nearer view of the possessed woman. The devil saluted him in a mocking tone: · Good-morning, Peter," said he, calling him also by his family name. " Come here and take a good view of me. Ah ! Peter, I know that you are a free-thinker; but, tell me, where were you last night ?" And then the devil related, in presence of every one in church, a shameful sin that Peter had committed the preceding night. He described all the circumstances with such precision that Peter was overwhelmed with confusion, and could not utter a word. " Yes," cried the devil in a mocking tone, " You have done it ; you dare not deny it."

Peter hurried away as fast as he could, muttering to himself : " The devil tells the truth this time. I thought that no one knew it but I myself and God."

Peter seemed to have forgotten that the devil is the witness of our evil actions, that he remembers them all well, and that, at the hour of death, he will bring them all against us, as he himself declared. " For it is thus," he added in a rage, " that I take revenge on sinners." Peter had not been to confession for many years, and, as a natural consequence, his morals were not exactly of the purest order. He had been guilty of gross sins which, in the fashionable world, go by the name of "pardonable weaknesses," "slight indiscretions," etc. The public accusation of the devil filled him with wholesome confusion. He rushed into the confessional, cast himself at the feet of the priest, confessed all his sins with true contrition, and received absolution. After having finished his confession, Peter had the boldness to press through the crowd once more; but this time he kept at a respectful distance from his infernal accuser. The exorcist saw Peter, and, knowing that he had been at confession, he told him to draw near. Then, pointing to him, the priest said to the devil: "See here, do you know this man?"

The devil raised his eyes, and leisurely surveyed Peter from head to foot, and from right to left. At last he said: "Why, really, it *is* Peter."

"Well!" said the priest, "do you know anything else about him?"

"No," answered the devil, "nothing else."

The devil then had no longer any knowledge of Peter's sins, because they had been entirely blotted out by the blood of Jesus Christ in the holy sacrament of confession.

We read of the holy Bishop Eligius that, desirous of attaining to a more exact purity of conscience, he made a general confession to a priest of all the sins he had committed from his earliest childhood, after which he began to advance with greater earnestness and fervor of spirit in the way of perfection.*

It is related in the life of St. Engelbert that, having retired to his private oratory in company with another bishop, he accused himself of all the sins he had committed with such a profusion of tears that they flowed down copiously over his breast, so that his confessor was no less edified than

* Surius *in Vita S. Eligii.*

182

astonished at the heartiness and intensity of his repentance. The next morning he resumed the confession of certain other of his failings, with a like abundance of tears.*

It is plain that this more lively repentance, this deeper, inward, and most real humility, must have more power to cleanse the soul, and help it to attain more speedily to purity of heart, especially as the purpose of amendment is commonly the more efficacious the greater our sorrow is for having offended Almighty God. St. Paul teaches that the supernatural sorrow works lasting fruits of salvation.† The apostle means to say that penance, when duly performed, produces a lasting amendment. Various reasons can be given for this. In the first place, the very disowning our faults and the good purposes of serious amendment which accompany a well-made general confession detach the soul from all affection for its past sins, and render it careful not to fall into them again. Then, again, the special grace bestowed in this sacrament strengthens the will in its conflict with our own disordered inclinations and the deceitful suggestions of our eternal foes. So that a general confession not only cleanses us from past failings, but makes us more watchful and careful not to commit them again.

St. Bernard, in his history of St. Malachy, relates that there was a woman so subject to fits of anger, rage, and fury that she seemed herself like a fury from the bottomless pit sent to torment every one who came in contact with her. Wherever she stayed her venomous tongue stirred up hatred and quarrelling, brawls and strife ; so that she became unbearable, not only to her own kindred and more immediate neighbors, but even to her very children, who, unable to live with her, had purposed to leave her and to go elsewhere. But, as a last endeavor, they took her to the holy Bishop Malachy, to see whether he would be able to tame the ungovernable temper of their mother. St. Malachy confined

* Surius in *Vita S. Engelberti*   † 2 Cor. vii. 10

183

himself to the enquiry whether she had ever confessed all her outbursts of passion, all her many outrageous words, and the numberless brawls she had provoked with her unruly tongue. She replied that she had not. "Well, then," continued the holy bishop, "confess them now to me." She did so, and after her confession he gave her some loving counsel, pointing out suitable remedies, and, having imposed a penance, absolved her from her sins. After this confession the woman, to the astonishment of all who knew her, appeared changed from the fierce lioness she had been into a meek lamb. St. Bernard concludes his narration by saying that "the woman was still living when he wrote, and that she, whose tongue had up to that time outraged and exasperated everybody, now seemed to be unable to resent the injuries, the insults, the mishaps, which daily fell to her lot." Behold, then, how a good general confession has power to cleanse the soul from past defilement, and to preserve it from falling again into grievous sin. In such a confession the source of sin is greatly weakened ; temptation ceases, or is altogether tempered ; grace is considerably increased ; the mind is unusually strengthened ; and the demon is enervated and confounded. Oh ! what consolation of mind results from this practice, what peace of conscience, what reformation of life, what confidence of pardon from God, what lightness of heart, what a change of person, what a facility in good works, what an increase in devotion, in tenderness of spirit, in vivacity of intelligence, in purity of conscience, and in all spiritual gifts which conduce to eternal salvation !

Christ Himself has been pleased to give us a striking illustration of this doctrine in the instance of that well known penitent, Blessed Margaret of Cortona. Beholding the fervent conversion of this once sinful woman, our Lord began to instruct and encourage her in divers ways, showing Himself to her overflowing with love and tender compas-

sion, and often addressing her as His "*poor little one!*"
One day the holy penitent, in a transport of that confidence
which is the natural fruit of filial love, said to Him, "O
my Lord! Thou always callest me Thy ' poor little one.'
Am I ever to have the happiness of hearing Thy divine lips
call me by the sweet name of ' my daughter' ? " " Thou
art not yet worthy of it," replied our dear Lord. " Before
thou canst receive the treatment and the name of daughter,
thou must more thoroughly cleanse thy soul by a general
accusation of all thy faults." On hearing this Margaret
applied herself to searching into her conscience, and during
eight successive days disclosed her sins to a priest, shedding
a torrent of tears at the same time. After her confession
she went to receive, in a most humble manner, the most
holy Body of our Lord. Scarce had she received it when
she heard most clearly in her inmost soul the words " My
daughter." At this most sweet name, to hear which she
had longed so ardently, she was rapt at once into an ecstasy,
and remained immersed, as it were, in an ocean of gladness
and delight. On recovering from her trance she began to
exclaim, as one beside herself, "O sweet word, 'My
daughter' ! O loving name ! O word full of joy !
O sound replete with assurance, 'My daughter' !"*
From this we may see how much a general confession, and
the preparation it implies, avail to cleanse, purify, and
beautify the soul ; since by means of it this holy woman
rose from the pitiable condition of a servant, in which she
was at the beginning of her conversion, to the honorable
rank of a well-beloved daughter. So that she who was at
first gazed upon by the Redeemer's pitying glances, was
afterwards contemplated by Him with love and most tender
complacency.

A Dominican novice, having one night fallen asleep near
the altar, heard a voice calling to him, "Go and have thy

* Francesco Marchese, *Vita di S. Margaretha da Cortona*, c. vii

tonsure renewed." On awaking the youth understood how God, by that voice, would have him confess his sins again. He went directly to cast himself at the feet of St. Dominic, and repeated his last confession with greater care and with more searching accuracy and diligence. Shortly after he retired to rest. In the midst of his slumbers he beheld an angel coming down from heaven, bearing in his hands a golden crown all set with priceless gems; and the angel, winging his flight towards him, placed this crown upon his head as an ornament to his brows. Let him who never made a general confession consider the above warning as made to himself. Let him take occasion of the approach of some special day or great festival, and say to himself, "Renew thy tonsure"; prepare for a general confession, which may cleanse thy soul, and render it wholly fair, bright, and pure in the sight of the Lord. Then he may confidently hope for the day when he will see himself crowned, not indeed in this life, but in the next, with a crown of resplendent stars.

Now, in order to preserve and increase the purity of soul, acquired by a good general. confession, we ought to have frequent recourse to the sacrament of penance.

Blosius tells us how our dear Saviour said one day to St. Bridget that in order to acquire His Spirit, and preserve the same when acquired, she should often confess her sins and imperfections to the priest.*

The greatest gift God can bestow upon a soul is the gift of divine love. This gift of perfect charity He bestows on the souls that are spotless and pure in His sight. He imparts this gift to the soul in proportion to her purity. It is certain that frequent confession is one of the most effectual means of speedily attaining to purity of soul, since, of its very nature, it helps us to acquire that clean-

---

* *Monit. Spirit.*, c. v.

ness of heart which is the crowning disposition foi re ceiving the gift of divine love.

"Blessed are the clean of heart." * Some have imag ned that cleanness of heart consists in an entire freedom from all sin and all imperfections whatsoever. But such cleanness of heart has been the privilege only of Jesus Christ and His ever-blessed Mother Mary. No one else can be said to have led so spotless a life in this polluted world as not to have contracted some stain. St. Thomas Aquinas says that a man can avoid each particular venial sin, but not all in general. And St. Leo the Great says of persons wholly devoted to God's service, that, owing to the frailty of our nature, not even such pious persons are free from the dust of trivial trangressions.†

Since, then, cleanness of heart cannot mean an entire freedom from sin, it must imply two things : First, an exact custody of our hearts, and a strict watchfulness over our outward actions, in order to avoid, as far as possible, the committing of a single wilful fault. The stricter the watch which a person keeps over his actions, and the more successful he is in diminishing the number of his failings, the more unblemished will be his purity.

Secondly, as, in spite of all the caution we can take, we shall ever be contracting some slight defilement of soul, it will be necessary to be constantly careful to cleanse our hearts from the impurities which accumulate through the more trivial faults into which we so frequently fall.

The cleanliness of a fine hall does not imply that no grain of dust shall ever fall upon the floor, walls, paintings, and furniture. Such cleanliness as this may not be locked for even in royal residences. It supposes only that the palace and its precincts be kept free from all accumulations of dirt, that all be often swept and dusted, and that everything opposed to cleanliness be removed. A lady, howevei

* Matt. v. + Serm. iv. De Quadr.

particular on the point of cleanliness, does not require that her garments should preserve their first whiteness, for that, she knows, is impossible ; but she is careful to keep them from all stain, and to have them frequently washed and cleansed from such stains as they may have contracted. The same holds good of purity of heart, which cannot, of course, consist in entire freedom from faults of every kind, but in carefully watching over self, in guarding against any wilful defilement, and in frequently purifying the conscience.

Now, these are precisely the two effects which frequent confession produces in the soul. Hence we attain, by its means, more speedily than by any other, to that purity of soul which is the crowning disposition for receiving divine love. Nothing in the world can cleanse our garments so completely from soil and spot as sacramental confession can purify our souls from every stain. In this sacrament the soul is all plunged into a bath of Christ's blood, which has a boundless efficacy for taking from it all that makes it hideous, and for rendering it whiter than the lily, purer than the driven snow. This is what the Apostle St. John assures us when he says, "If we confess our sins, God is faithful and just to forgive us our sins, and to cleanse us from all iniquity.*

Bodily medicine, if very sparingly used, gives relief, it is true, while, if frequently applied, it restores or preserves health ; thus too confession, if made even but seldom, produces saving effects in the soul, while, if made frequently, it begets in it the fulness of perfection.

To this may be added another most important reflection : it is that confession, made frequently, is a most effectual means of disarming our ghostly enemy, and thus disabling him from doing us injury and hindering our spiritual progress. It is easy to account for this, since all the power which the enemy has over us comes from the sins that we

* 1 John i. 9

commit. If these be mortal, they put him in full possession of our souls ; if venial, though they do not confer a dominion on him, yet they embolden him to attack us with greater violence. It thence follows that if we confess duly and frequently, the soul will be habitually free from sin ; and thus the devil will be deprived of all dominion over us, and will have no courage or power to harm us ; so that we shall be more free and unshackled in our pilgrimage towards heaven.

Cæsarius relates * that a theologian of blameless life, being about to die, beheld the devil lurking in a corner of his room ; and he addressed the fiend in the words of St. Martin : " What art thou doing here, thou cruel beast ? " He then, by virtue of his priestly power, commanded the devil to declare what it was that most injured him and his fellows in this world. Though thus adjured, the devil remained silent. Not allowing himself to be baffled, the priest conjured the demon, in the name of God, to answer him, and answer him with truth. The evil spirit thereupon made this reply : " There is nothing in the Church which does us so much harm, which so unnerves our power, as frequent confession." Hence whoever aspires to cleanness of heart, and to perseverance in it, should make a general confession, and then confess often and see that his confessions are good.

* *Mirac.*, lib. ii. c. xxxviii.

MARY, MOTHER OF MERCY

CHAPTER X.

A FATHER had in store costly presents of gold and jewels which he intended to give his children as a token of his love for them. The time chosen by the father for the bestowal of his gifts, as being best calculated to make a deep impression on the minds of his children, was when he lay on his death-bed. Thus the gifts became the last memorials of his love.

Our divine Saviour thought and acted in the same manner when hanging on the cross. We can imagine Him to say : "I have already given men so many proofs of my love towards them. I have created them. I preserve their lives. I have become man for their sake. I have lived among them for more than thirty years. I have given them my own flesh and blood as food and drink for their souls. I am yet to suffer and die for them on this cross, that I may reopen heaven to them. What more can I do for them ? I can make them one more present. I will give them a most precious gift : the only gift that is still left, so that they may not be able to charge me with having done less for them than I might have done. I have kept this gift to the last, because it is my desire that they should ever remember it ; because it is so precious in my sight, so dear to my heart, so necessary for all those who will believe in me : and because it is to be the means of preserving all the other gifts. This last gift, this keepsake of my most tender love for men, is my own most pure Virgin Mother."

God alone knows the inmost yearnings of the human heart. God alone can fully understand and compassionate our weakness. At our birth to this natural life God gave each of us a father and a mother, to be our guide and support, our refuge and consolation ; and when, in the holy sacrament of baptism, we were come again to the true life of grace, God gave us also a Father and a Mother. He taught us to call Him " Our Father, who art in heaven." He gave us His own blessed Virgin Mother to be our true and loving Mother. That Mary is our Mother we were told by Jesus Himself when hanging on the cross: " Behold thy Mother." * By His all-powerful word God created the heavens and the earth ; by His word He changed water into wine at the wedding-feast ; by His word He gave life to the dead ; by His word He changed bread and wine into His own body and blood ; and by the same word He made His own beloved Mother to be truly and really our Mother also· Mary, then, is our Mother, as Jesus willed and declared ; and Mary, our Mother, is an all-powerful Mother ; she is an all-merciful Mother.

God alone is all-powerful by nature, but Mary is all-powerful by her prayers. What more natural than this ?

Mary is made Mater Dei, the Mother of God. Behold two words, the full meaning of which can never be com prehended either by men or angels. To be Mother of God is, as it were, an infinite dignity ; for the dignity of that Mother is derived from the dignity of her Son. As there can be no son of greater excellence than the Son of God, so there can be no mother greater than the Mother of God. Hence St. Thomas asks whether God could make creatures nearer perfection than those already created, and he answers yes, He can, except three : i.e., 1, The Incarnation of the Son of God ; 2, The maternity of the Blessed Virgin Mary ; and 3, The everlasting beatitude ; in other words, God can create numberless worlds, all different from one another in beauty, but He cannot make anything greater

* John xix. 27.

than the Incarnation of Christ, the Mother of God, and the happiness of the blessed in heaven. And why can he not ? Because God Himself is involved in and most intimately united to each of these works, and is their object. (" Haec tria Deum involvunt et pro objecto habent.") As there can be no man as perfect as Christ, because He is a Man-God, and as there can be no greater happiness than the beatific vision and enjoyment and possession of God in heaven, where the soul is, as it were, transformed into God and most inseparably united to His nature, so also no mother can be made as perfect as the Mother of God. These three works are of a certain infinite dignity on account of their intimate union with God, the infinite Good. There can then be nothing better, greater than, or as perfect as, these three works, because there can be nothing better than God Himself. The Blessed Virgin gave birth to Christ, who is the natural Son of God the Father, both as God and as man. Christ, then, as man, is the natural Son both of the Blessed Virgin and of God the Father. Behold in what intimate relation she stands with the Blessed Trinity, she having brought forth the same Son whom God the Father has generated from all eternity.

Moreover, the Blessed Virgin is the Mother of God, who had no earthly father ; she was both mother and father to Jesus Christ. Hence she is the Mother of God far more than others are the mothers of men ; for Christ received of the Blessed Virgin alone his whole human nature, and is indebted to his Mother for all that he is as man. Hence Christ, by being conceived and born of the Blessed Virgin, became in a certain sense her debtor, and is under more obligations to her for being to Him both mother and father than other children are to their parents.

If Mary is the Mother of God, what wonder, then, that God has glorified and will glorify, through all ages, her power of intercession with Him and her mercy for all men ?

The Eternal Father has chosen Mary to be the mother of His only Son ; the Holy Spirit chose her as His spouse. The Son, who has promised a throne in heaven to the apostles who preached His word, is bound in justice to do more for the Mother who bore Him, the eternal Word. If we believe in honoring our mother, surely He believes in honoring and glorifying His. Now, what honors, what prerogatives, should God bestow on her, whom he has so much favored, and who served Him so devotedly ! How should she be honored whom the King of Heaven deigns to honor !

A king was once in great danger of being assassinated but a faithful subject discovered the plot, revealed it, and thus saved the monarch's life. The king was moved with gratitude, and asked his ministers, " How could he be honored whom the king desires to honor ? " One of his ministers replied, " He whom the king desired to honor should be clad in kingly robes ; he should be crowned with a kingly diadem, and the first of the royal princes should go before him and cry aloud, ' Thus shall he be honored whom the king desires to honor.' " In this manner did an earthly king reward him who saved his life. And how should the King of heaven and earth reward her who gave Him His human life ? How should Jesus reward the loving Mother who bore Him, nursed Him, saved Him in his infancy from a most cruel death ? Is there any honor too high for her whom God Himself has so much honored ? Is there any glory too dazzling for her whom the God of glory has chosen for His dwelling-place ? No ; it is God's own decree : Let her be clad in royal robes. Let the fulness of the Godhead so invest her, so possess her, that she shall be a spotless image of the sanctity, the beauty, the glory of God Himself. Let her be crowned with a kingly diadem. Let her reign for ever as the peerless Queen of heaven, of earth, and of hell. Let her reign as the Mother of mercy, the Consoler of the afflicted, the Refuge of sinners. Let the first of the royal princes walk before her. Let the angels, the prophets, the apostles, the martyrs, let all the saints, kiss the hem of her garment and rejoice in the honor of being the servants of the Mother of God.

No wonder, then, if we rarely hear of Mary but in connection with a miraculous demonstration of the power of God. She was conceived as no other human being ever was conceived. She again conceived her Son and God in a miraculous manner; miracles attended her visit to her cousin St. Elizabeth ; the birth of her divine Child was accompanied by many striking prodigies. When she carried Him in her arms to present Him in the Temple, behold new miracles followed her steps. The first miracle of her divine Son was performed at her request. She took part in the awful mystery of the Passion. She shared in the sevenfold gifts of the Holy Spirit at Pentecost. In a word, miracles seem to have been the order in her life, the absence of miracles the exception ; so that we are as little surprised to find them attend her everywhere as we should be astonished to hear of them in connection with ourselves. Mary was a living miracle. All that we know of her miraculous power now is but little when compared with the prodigies which were effected through her agency during her earthly career. She saluted her cousin Elizabeth ; and when that holy woman " heard her salutation, she was filled with the Holy Ghost." She addressed her divine Son at the marriage-feast, and said, " They have no more wine "; and immediately the filial charity which had bound Him to her for thirty years constrained Him to comply with her request. He whose meat and drink it was to do the will of His heavenly Father seemed to make the will of Mary the law of His action rather than His own. Again, there was a moment when the mystery of the Incarnation hung upon the word of her lips : the destiny of the world depended upon an act of her will. When God wished to create the world, " He spoke and it was done "; when He wished to redeem the world, He left it to the consent of His creature, and that creature was Mary. She said, " Be it done to me according to Thy word," and the miracle of all miracles, the mystery of all mysteries, was consummated. " God was made flesh, and dwelt amongst us."

It cannot surprise us, then, that she should continue to be a centre of miraculous action. Her whole previous history prepares us for this. It seems to be the law of her being; she represents to us the most stupendous miracle that the world ever witnessed. It seems, therefore, almost natural that she should be able to suspend here and there the course of natural events by the power of her intercession. All that we know of her miraculous power now is as nothing when compared with the prodigies which were effected through her agency during her earthly career, and which we must believe, unless we would forfeit the very name of Christian. The apostles did not enter upon their office of intercession till the coming of the Holy Spirit at Pentecost; after that, whatever they should ask the Father in Christ's name they were certain to receive. Mary began her office of inter-cession at Cana. Its commencement was inaugurated by Christ's first miracle. It is true that His answer, in words at least, seemed at first unfavorable. But only observe how every circumstance of that event strengthens the Catholic view of our Lord's conduct. Mary's faith in her Son's power, and in His willingness to grant her request, never wavered, even when He seemed to make a difficulty. Whether His words had a meaning wholly different from that ordinarily attached to them now, or whether she, whose heart was as His own, read His consent in the tone of His voice or in the glance of His eye, her only answer was the words addressed to the servants : " Whatever He shall say to you, do it," evidently proving that she never for an in-stant doubted the favorable issue of her request. Now, if what appeared to be an unseasonable exercise of Mary's influence resulted in a miracle, and the first of the public miracles of our Lord; and if He predicted the coming of an hour when the exercise of her influence should no longer be unseasonable, as His words clearly imply, what prodigies must not her intercession effect at the present time! If she could thus prevail with God in her lowliness, what can she not obtain now in her exalted state! Number, if you can, those who, through the intercession of Mary, have been restored to life; how many sick have been cured; how many captives have been set at liberty; how many have been delivered by Mary who were in danger of perishing by fire, in danger of shipwreck, in danger of war and pestilence! Number all the kingdoms which she has founded; all the empires which she has preserved; to how many armies that put themselves under her protection has she not given victory over their enemies! Call to mind Narses, the general of the Emperor Justinian. Was it not through Mary that he gained the victory over the Goths? And was not the victory of Heraclius over the Persians due to Mary? Pelagius I. sought her aid, and slew 80,000 Saracens. Basil the Emperor defeated the Saracens by her assistance. By the same assistance Godfrey de Bouillon defeated the Saracens and regained Jerusalem. Through her Alfonsus VIII., King of Castile, slew 200,000 Moors, with the loss of scarcely twenty or thirty Christians. Pius V. obtained through her intercession the celebrated victory over the Turks at Lepanto. How many heresies has she not crushed! It was she who animated St. Athanasius and St. Gregory Thaumaturgus to defend the Church against the Arians. It was she who animated St. Cyrillus to defend the doctrine of the Church against the Nestorians. It was she who inspired St. Augustine to raise his voice against the Pelagians. It was she who encouraged St. John Damascene to attack the fierce heresy of the Iconoclasts. It was she who animated

197

St. Dominic to defend the doctrines of the Church against the Albigenses. It was she who filled St. Ignatius Loyola with undaunted courage to battle against the baneful heresy of Luther. It was she who inspired St. Alphonsus de Liguori to take up arms against the poisonous serpents of Jansenism and Gallicanism. It is she who has inspired so many persons to consecrate themselves to the service of God in the religious and apostolic life.

These public manifestations of her power recorded in the history of the Church are indeed wonderful ; but her secret influence—the influence which she exerts over the hearts of men, over human passions and motives of action, over the invisible enemies of our salvation—is even more wonderful, more comprehensive still. This influence is felt through the whole Church ; it is of hourly occurrence. Those who have felt its gentle operation can bear witness to the truth of its existence. How many of the just have become perfect through Mary ; how many there are who have received the grace of purity through her ; how many there are who have obtained through her the grace to overcome their passions ; how many who have already obtained through her the crown of life everlasting ! Behold a St. Augustine, a St. John Damascene, a St. Germanus, a St. Anselm, a St. Bonaventure, a St. Bernard, a St. Dominic, a St. Vincent Ferrer, a St. Xavier, a St. Alphonsus ; behold the countless multitude of saints who for their sanctity have shone like suns in the heavens. Was it not through Mary that they became holy ? Have they passed through any other gate than through that opened by Mary ? Think of all the sinners who have been converted through Mary. The hourly conversions of such numbers are the hourly triumphs of Mary's power ; they are the secret but most conclusive evidence of the queenly authority with which she is invested for the welfare of all men.

Some years ago a mission was given in a certain town,

The people took great interest in the exercises, and approached the sacraments with great fervor. There was one, however, who took no part in the mission. He had not been to confession for over twenty years. He led a very immoral life, and, as a natural consequence, had become an infidel. Not satisfied with being corrupt himself, he tried to ruin all around him. He even spent large sums of money in buying bad books, which he distributed freely amongst the young people of his neighborhood. He spared no means which wealth and cunning could devise to ruin pure and innocent souls. On the last day of the mission, whilst the missionaries were all busily engaged in hearing confessions, this unhappy man came to church also, and entered one of the confessionals. He began to tell his sins one after the other. He accused himself of the most enormous crimes, but he told them without the least sign of sorrow—nay, he even gloried in his wickedness; especially when he had related how cunningly he had devised his plans, how well he had succeeded in destroying innocent souls, he would pause for a moment and look at the priest with an air of triumph, as if to say: " Now, was not that well done ? " He went on thus relating his sins for about three-quarters of an hour ; at last he stopped and said : " Now, sir, I suppose I have told you enough for the present ! " The poor missionary had listened patiently to the wretched man without even once interrupting him, and now he was in the greatest strait, as he did not know what to do with him. Should he give this hardened sinner absolution, and thereby load his soul with another mortal sin—the sin of sacrilege—or should ne send him away with that frightful load of sin still weighing upon his soul ? What was to be done ? At last the priest began to exhort him to repentance. He spoke to him of the enormity of sin, the terrors of judgment, the torments of hell; but the man interrupted him, and said in an insolent tone: " Oh ! let all that go for the present. That may do very well to frighten old women. I know it is a part of your trade to talk thus, but you see such things do not affect me." The priest continued, however, to exhort him, but the man interrupted him again, and said : " My good sir, you are only wasting words. I do not even ask for absolution. If you wish to absolve me, very good ; if not, I am quite satisfied. It matters little to me whether you absolve me or not." The priest reflected and prayed for a moment, and then said to the hardened sinner : " Well, my good friend, at least one thing you will grant : that I have listened to you very patiently." " Yes, that is true," answered the man. " In fact, I was astonished and I must say even disappointed, at it myself. I expected that you would scold me and fly into a passion ; and, to tell the truth, that was just what I wanted." " Well, then," said the priest, " since I have done you the favor of listening to you so patiently, will you also do me a little favor ? " " Well," said the man, "if it is not too much or too costly, perhaps I might do it." " No ! " said the priest ; " the favor I ask will cost you nothing. You have told me, among other things, that you often said publicly that the Blessed Virgin Mary is nothing more than any ordinary woman. Now go yonder to the Blessed Virgin's altar, and say slowly, three times, these words : ' O Mary ! I believe that you have no more power than any ordinary woman ; if you have, then prove it to me.' " With these words the priest sent him away, and continued to hear other confessions. About an hour after a man was seen drawing near the confessional with a slow, heavy tread. It was the same sinner again, but oh ! how changed. He threw himself on his knees before the priest, but could not speak ; his voice was choked by sobs and tears, his strong frame quivered with emotion. " O father ! " cried he at last, " is there any hope for me ? Oh ! what a monster I have been ! Father, forgive me for having insulted you awhile ago ; for having dishonored the holy sacrament of confession. Ah ! now I wish to make a good, sincere confession. I wish to change my life, and I wish to atone for all the evil I have ever done." You may imagine now great was the joy of the priest at witnessing this happy charge. He enquired of the man the cause of his sudden conversion. "Father," said the now repentant sinner, "I did as you told me ; I went to the Blessed Virgin's altar and said : ' O Mary ! I believe . . .' Father, I cannot say those wicked words again. Scarcely had I uttered them when a strange feeling came over me which I could not resist. All the sins of my whole life, my black ingratitude to God, appeared in an instant before me. My heart, my inmost soul, was wrung with poignant grief. I could not help it, I burst into tears—tears of true repentance ; and now, father, I kneel here before you to obtain forgiveness for my enormous crimes." The missionary absolved him, and his heart was filled with joy as he received back the prodigal son who had been straying away for so many years. Next morning this man knelt at the communion-rail for the first time in twenty years. And when the good parish priest saw him there kneeling with the rest, he was so overcome with emotion that he had to turn away his face to hide his tears. The day after the mission all the clergy and the leading members of the congregation had assembled in the house of the parish priest. As they were speaking together, a knock was heard at the door ; the door was opened, and in walked the convert. He fell on his knees before the parish priest ; he kissed his hands, and even his feet, and said, with tears in his eyes : "Father, forgive me for having so often grieved your fatherly heart by my sinful conduct. Father, forgive me !" Then he turned to all those present, and, on his knees, begged their forgiveness for the bad example he had given ; after which he arose, and, raising his right hand to heaven, cried : "I swear by the living God that I will consecrate the rest of my life to God's service. With God's assistance I will repair, to the best of my power, all the evil I have done, all the scandal I have given." And this man kept his word. Long after, the parish priest wrote to one of the missionaries that this man, who had formerly led so scandalous a life, was now a source of edification to the whole community ; that he spared no pains and shunned no labor whenever anything was to be done for the glory of God and the salvation of souls.

Nothing is too great for Mary's power. And as there is nothing too great for her power, so there is nothing too insignificant for her notice. While she fights the battles of the universal Church, she cares for the salvation of the least of Christ's little ones. She is always ready to console and refresh their fainting spirits, to procure for them even the smallest actual grace. From the holy virgin martyr who in the first ages of the Church invoked the aid of Mary against the demon of impurity to the youth who kneels to-day before her altar, imploring the preservation of his inno-cence or the restoration of lost virtue, it has never been heard that any one who fled to her protection, implored her assistance, or asked her prayers was left unheeded. One, for instance, sets his heart upon obtaining from the Blessed Virgin the recovery or conversion of a dear friend ; another prays for the clear manifestation of the divine will in his regard at some critical period of his life ; another prays for some special favor ; they begin a novena to Mary, and ere it is ended their prayer is heard. In the daily strife with sin and temptation the name of Mary acts as a spell upon the spirits of evil. If men at times give way to pride and con-tempt of others, they invoke the aid of Mary, and their hearts become kind and humble. Does the thought of im-purity cross their mind, they call upon her name ; they raise their eyes towards her throne, and the demon flies from them. Whilst Mary, this loving Mother, was yet on earth, her heart was always full of mercy and compassion towards all men. Destined from all eternity to be the Mother of the God of mercy, Mary received a heart like unto the heart of her divine Son Jesus—a heart that was free from every stain of sin and overflowing with burning charity. Yes, Mary's mercy grew up with her from her tender childhood, and compassion became with her a second nature. See, she herself reveals the loving mercy that burns in her heart. In the little house at Nazareth, in her silent chamber, she is kneeling all alone. With more than seraphic ardor, she implores God to send speedily the long-wished-for Redeemer. The angel enters and salutes Mary: "Hail, full of grace." He announces the glad tidings that God Himself desires to call her " Mother," and waits for her answer. The whole human race, sinful and sorrowful, lies prostrate at her feet. God Himself, the Creator of all things, awaits the free consent of His own creature. And now Mary reveals all her virtues, displays her unbounded mercy. The decisive moment has come ; Mary becomes a mother, and remains a spotless virgin. She becomes the Queen of Heaven, and remains the meek and lowly handmaid. She utters the merciful "*fiat.*" It is for us that she utters it. " Be it done to me according to Thy word." By the divine "*fiat*" this world was called out of nothingness into existence, and by the "*fiat*" of Mary this same world, dead in sin, was recalled to the life of grace. Well does Mary know what this consent will cost her ; but her great love for us, her great mercy towards us sinners, impels her, and she willingly offers herself to suffer sorrow and contempt, to endure every pang, for our sake.

Behold once more this holy Virgin, full of divine grace and mercy, going in haste over the mountains of Judea. See how she undertakes a long and tedious journey of several days —and all for what ? Her compassionate heart knows that the infant John the Baptist lies bound by the chains of sin ; she hastens to burst those fetters. No sooner has Mary arrived at the house of Elizabeth than the infant is freed from sin, is sanctified, and the compassionate Virgin sings a sublime canticle of praise and gladness.

The evangelist tells us in a few words the entire fulness of the mercy of Mary: "Mary, of whom was born Jesus." These few words contain such a superabundance of graces for us that we can think of nothing better, we can think of nothing greater. For Jesus is our most merciful Redeemer. He is mercy itself, and Mary is the Mother of Jesus—the Mother of mercy. The shepherds of Bethlehem can tell, and the wise men of the East can bear witness to the fact, that when they found the Child and its Mother in the poor and lowly stable, their joy, their happiness, their consolation knew no bounds.

If we wish to see still more clearly how deeply the heart of Mary felt for our miseries, let us approach the Temple and see Mary offer up her dearly-beloved Son for us. Yes, so dearly has Mary loved the world that she has sacrificed her only-begotten Son for the life of the world. Only he who understands the boundless love that Mary bore to her divine Son can fully understand the love and mercy of Mary towards us, her erring children.

The love and solicitude with which Mary watched over the infant Jesus was also love and solicitude for us. It was for us that she nourished Jesus, in order that the blood which she gave Him might be shed for us and for our sins; it was for us that she nourished Jesus, in order that He might grow up and labor for our salvation ; it was for us that she saved her divine Infant from the hands of the cruel Herod, in order that He might enrich us with His doctrine and example, and that He might finally lay down His life for us upon the cross.

"Beside the cross of Jesus stood his Mother." Only think, such a mother witnessing such a death—the death of her Only-Begotten ! Christian mothers who have stood by the bedside of a dying child may realize the anguish of such a scene. But it was even here that the greatest blessing was bestowed on us; for it was here that Mary was first publicly proclaimed to be our Mother. "Woman, behold thy son!" "Dear Mother," said her dying Son, "I am now about to die; I am about to depart from thee, but I leave thee another son in my stead; I leave thee my beloved disciple. Thou shalt now be his Mother; thou shalt now be the Mother, the Refuge, of sinners. Woman, behold thy son!" Mark well those words! Ye angels of heaven, bear witness to those words! Jesus has provided for us in His testament. He has bequeathed to us a priceless treasure. He has given us His own pure Virgin Mother. And, indeed, Mary receives us as her children. Every word of her divine Son is sacred in her eyes. She knows that such is the will of her dying Son. The will is written in blood— in the blood of Jesus—and sealed by His death. Jesus finally returns to heaven, and Mary remains yet on earth to encourage and console His sorrowing disciples. And now that Mary also has ascended into heaven, has she forgotten those children of sorrow whom Jesus has confided to her care? Oh no; it is not in our Mother's heart to forget her children. Never did any one ask a grace of Mary without being heard. In heaven her love and mercy towards us has only become more ardent, more efficacious. Every century, nay, every year, every day, every hour, especially the dying hour of so many sinners, bears witness to Mary's undying love and inexhaustible mercy.

St. Teresa gives us an account of a merchant of Valladolid who did not live as a good Christian should live. However, he had some devotion to the Blessed Virgin. One day St. Teresa went to Valladolid to find a house for her nuns. The merchant, hearing that Teresa was seeking a house, went to her and offered to give her one of his houses, saying that he would give it in honor of the Blessed Virgin

Mary. St. Teresa thanked him and took the house. Two months after, the gentleman was suddenly taken so very ill that he was not able to speak or to make his confession. He could only show by signs that he wished to beg pardon of our Lord for his sins, and died soon after. "After his death," says St. Teresa, "I saw our Lord. He told me that this gentleman had been very near losing his soul. But He had mercy on him because of the service he did to His blessed Mother by giving the house in her honor. She obtained for him, in the hour of death, the grace of true contrition for his sins." "I was glad," says St. Teresa, "that this soul was saved; for I was very much afraid it would have been lost on account of his bad life."

Ah! how great is the power and mercy of Mary! How kind, how solicitous, how merciful, how careful and compassionate is the Mother of God! How often are we ignorant of the troubles that await us! Mary, however, knows them, and hastens to our assistance. How often are we unconscious of the dangers that surround us! Mary perceives them, and protects us from all harm. How often does this good Mother pray for us when we do not think of asking her prayers! Let us treasure up those words in our hearts: "Dear Son, they have no wine." They will console us in the hour of affliction. When a sense of utter loneliness oppresses us, when we seem abandoned by all the world, then is the time to remember that we have a Mother in heaven. The Blessed Virgin Mary has not forgotten us. How often has she already prayed for us to her divine Son: "My dear Son, see, my servant has no more wine. See, he stands sorely in need of the virtue of a lively faith, charity, and holy purity." How often has Mary changed the waters of pain and sorrow into the cheering wine of joy and gladness! When we stood on the brink of the precipice, and stretched forth our hands to sin, Mary, like a tender mother, stretched forth her arms to save us. When, by our sins, we cruelly pierced the Sacred Heart of Jesus, then it was that Mary offered up for us the precious blood that gushed forth from the gaping wound.

If God has endowed the Blessed Mother of His only-begotten Son with such power and dominion, and with such charity and mercy towards us, is it strange that we rejoice in the name, in the dignity, in the glory, in the power, and mercy of Mary? Would it not, on the contrary, be strange indeed, were we to be slow in proclaiming her praise, and power and mercy? Her first and strongest title to our love, homage, and confidence in her is the indelible character of glory communicated to her by the miracle of the Incarnation, by which God became man of her substance, the Eternal became subject to the laws of time and space, the Infinite was comprehended in the form of an infant, the invisible Creator of the universe became visible to the eyes of His creatures. Her co-operation was necessary before that miracle could take place ; a portion of its splendor, therefore, rests for ever on her royal head. She has earned for herself, through her correspondence with God's grace, new titles of honor and renown ; but the mystery of the Incarnation lies at the foundation of her greatness. With that mystery, which is continued in a certain sense in the most holy Sacrament of the Altar, she too is intimately connected, inasmuch as the sacred humanity which we worship there, in union with the divinity of Jesus Christ, was assumed from her virginal flesh and blood.

St. Anselm, St. Francis, St. Bonaventure, St. Peter Damian, St. Bernard, and, in these latter days, St. Alphonsus, stand as witnesses to the great spiritual law that the love of the Virgin Mother of God is not a sentiment or a poetry in religion, which may or may not be encouraged by individuals at their will, but that love and veneration second only to the love and veneration paid to her divine Son, is due to her by a law which springs from the very sub stance of the faith. It is impossible to realize the Incarnation as we ought, and not to love and venerate the Mother of God; it is impossible to love the Son without loving the Mother. In proportion to our love to the Son will be our love to the Mother who bore Him; in so far as we are conformed to the likeness of the Son we shall love the Mother, who, next to the Eternal Persons, the Father and the Holy Ghost, is the dearest object of the love of the Eternal Son. The love of the Mother of God is the overflow of the love we bear to her divine Son; it descends from Him to her, and we may measure our love to Him by our love to her. It is impossible to be cold, distant, dry, or reserved towards the Mother of our Redeemer, and to be fervent in our love to the Redeemer Himself. Such as we are to Him, such, in due measure, shall we be to her.

Not to love and honor Mary sincerely must proceed either from culpable neglect or from want of faith in the divine revelation and in the wise plans of Providence. ' He that despiseth you despiseth me," said our Blessed Lord to His apostles. His words apply with greater force to His holy Mother; and, " He that despiseth me despiseth Him that sent me." Far from us be the unworthy fear that by having recourse to Mary we should disparage the honor of Christ. The more we look up to her, the higher must her divine Son rise in our regard; for His glory exceeds hers as the inherent splendor of the sun surpasses the borrowed light of the moon, as the divine Creator excels His most gifted creature. We cannot love, and honor, and pray to Mary without loving and honoring Him who has made her so worthy of love. And we cannot love Him as He ought to be loved without being especially drawn towards His Blessed Mother. If we love Him, we must imitate Him to the best of our power, especially in His filial love and reverence for His Blessed Mother.

The saints have always made Christ's love for His Blessed

Mother the model of their love for that most holy Virgin. To name the saints who were deeply devoted to Mary would be to name them all. The more they strove to love God, the more they felt drawn to love Mary; or, to speak more correctly, the more they increased in love of Mary, the more they increased also in love for God.

The Church has never grown weary of praising and honoring Mary. Consider the many days in the year that are consecrated to her honor; the solemnity and frequency of her feasts. The hymns composed in honor of her are numberless. She is extolled by the clergy, revered by all nations, esteemed and honored by all that are of good-will and truly sincere heart. But whoever would conceive a true idea of the power and mercy of the Blessed Virgin Mary, whoever would fairly estimate the heart-felt loyalty of Christians for their heavenly Queen and Mother, must pass into Catholic lands and observe the fervent multitudes that crowd the sanctuaries of Our Blessed Lady. Mindful of the many extraordinary favors received from Mary in some particular sanctuary of hers, the people call upon Our Lady of Loretto, Our Lady of Einsiedeln, Our Lady of Fourvière, Our Lady of Puy, Our Lady of La Salette, Our Lady of Lourdes, Maria Zell, Our Lady of Guadalupe, and a hundred others. All Europe is filled with sanctuaries of Our Blessed Lady. There sacred processions sweep through the streets; long trains of pilgrims wind by the banks of rivers or through the greenwood to a favored chapel of Our Lady. The sweet face of the Virgin Mother smiles upon them as they pass the wayside shrine; the hum of business is stilled, and the traveller bares his head for a moment's communion with God, as the angelus bell rings from the neighboring steeple; and the very mile stones on the roadside become niches which speak to us of love and devotion to Mary.

It is impossible for those who have never visited the

towns and villages of a Catholic country to conceive the feeling of delight with which the pious traveller is affected at the sight of so many images of the Blessed Virgin placed at the corners of streets, in squares and public places, on bridges, fountains, and obelisks, or between the stalls of a village market or fair. Each statue or holy image has its lantern, and is decorated with flowers, which the people of the neighborhood renew every morning at daybreak. The sweet name of Mary is the most familiar of household words. The poet chants her praises; the painter and sculptor, the masters of art, love to reproduce her pure, maternal face; and even the Protestant has not yet learned to speak of her with disrespect nor utterly banish all love for her from his heart. It is on account of this great love for the Blessed Mother of God that there is not a province but has its own favorite image and sanctuary of Our Lady, and, linked with that image, some legend which marks the spot as a chosen abode, selected for the outpourings of her maternal favors.

From the firm belief that such spots are more highly favored than others, and that prayers offered there are more readily heard, the pious practice has risen of making public or private pilgrimages to these holy places, in order to obtain some particular favor, or to render thanks to God, through His Blessed Mother, for favors obtained. For if God sends us so many favors through Mary as their channel —the channel naturally the most agreeable to Him—we are impelled to return our thanks through the same blessed channel. When our hearts are filled with emotions of gratitude or veneration, we naturally seek to give vent to our feelings by some outward act of devotion; and hence the faithful have, in all ages, formed solemn processions, made long pilgrimages, to some favorite shrine of the Madonna, in order to express their love and devotion to their beloved Queen.

In these sanctuaries of Our Blessed Lady may be seen votive offerings, ornaments of gold and silver and precious stones, in commemoration of miraculous cures or other extraordinary favors obtained through the intercession of Mary by those who invoked her at her holy shrine. The blind are restored to sight, the lame walk, the dead are raised to life, demons are expelled from the bodies of men. These are authentic facts, attested not only by persons of note who have heard them from others, but by thousands of eye-witnesses whose sincerity we cannot doubt—facts so numerous that, if all were written, the world itself could scarcely contain the books ; facts which plainly tell us that since God is pleased to assist us in all our necessities, spiritual and temporal, through Mary, it is also in Mary that we are to seek and to find our constant help or intercessor in the work of our sanctification and salvation. If we consider how the anti-Catholic pulpit and lecture-room, the press and every public resort, re-echo against the Catholic Church the false charges of idolatry, of taking from God the honor due to Him alone, and giving it to a creature ; if we consider how even the most charitable of our enemies shake their heads and bewail what they call the unfortunate propensity of the Roman Catholics to give too much honor to Mary ; if we consider how many temptations surround the Catholic here, how hard it is to bear contempt, misrepresentation, and wilful falsehood ; how much easier it is to hide a delicate and beloved sentiment than to expose it to the risk of a sneer ; how swift the pace of the money-hunter is here ; how little the beautiful in life and faith is cultivated ; and how devoted men are to what they are pleased to call the practical—which means simply more careful diligence for the body than for the soul, for time than for eternity—if we consider all this, the wonder is not that there is so much or so little devotion to Our Lady, but that there is any devotion at all. Yet it is safe to believe that notwithstanding all these difficulties, there is no Catholic country in Europe, there never has been a country, in which reverent love and earnest, heart-felt devotion for the Blessed Mother of God are more deeply rooted, more ardently cherished, or more fervently practised than in this country of America. This devotion to Mary guides and influences the hearts of men, and it is found pure and glowing in the souls even of those who seem to be most engrossed in worldly affairs. It begins in earliest childhood, when the scapular and the medal are placed around the neck of the babe, to remain there even to the hour of death. As the child grows up, he associates himself with some sodality of the Blessed Virgin. As soon as he has grown up to manhood he joins some benevolent society which is placed under the special patronage of the Queen of Angels. The Daughters of Our Lady of the Visitation of Loretto and similar communities train up our young girls; the Brothers of Mary devote themselves to the education of our youth. The bishop labors patiently till his seminary of St. Mary is completed; the priest toils arduously until his parish of the Annunciation or of the Assumption is established; all join their prayers, their counsel, their wealth, their labor, their self-denial, until the cross peers through the greenwood from the convent of Mary's Help, till the church of the Immaculate crowns the summit of the hill.

In the council held in Baltimore, in 1846, the assembled fathers—twenty-two bishops with their theologians—solemnly chose the Blessed Virgin Immaculate as Patroness of the United States of America. These Fathers of the council had been trained to honor the Blessed Mother of God; they had labored in her service; they desired to add this crowning glory to all that they had done in her honor during a long life of labor and prayer; they wished at the same time to show their zeal for the true interests of this country by placing the entire United States under her protection in this solemn and public manner. In the following year this election was confirmed by the Sovereign Pontiff, and from that time, in all public sessions that close these august assemblies, after the " Te Deum " has been chanted, the cantors, richly vested, stand before the altar and intone their first acclamation to the Most High. As soon as that solemn hymn of praise is ended, they burst forth in the words " Beatissimæ Virgini Mariæ, sine labe originali conceptæ, harum Provinciarum Patronæ honor æternus." Translated: " To the most Blessed Virgin Mary, conceived without original sin, the patron of these provinces, be eternal honor." And in chorus the venerable bishops, the theologians and attendant priests, and the whole multitude of the people repeat the glad acclamation.

Ever since that solemn act Mary has gained vast possessions in this country; and we may confidently hope that she will conquer it all and annex it all to the kingdom of her divine Son. Love and devotion towards Mary are on the increase. This love for the Mother of God is a good omen; she will not fail to show openly that she is the Patroness of this country and the Perpetual Help of all who invoke her holy name. As she selected, in Europe, certain spots as resting-places for the outpourings of her maternal affection, so she will do the same in those cities and towns of these United States where the faithful truly love her and invoke her as the Perpetual Help in all temptations and troubles. In fact, in our own days, in these States, the Blessed Virgin has bestowed extraordinary favors ; she has performed miracles in support of the truth, already so often repeated, that she is Our Lady of Perpetual Help here as well as in Europe.

This is the Mother whose equal is not to be found—the Blessed Mother of God, the Immaculate Virgin Mary. It is to this most loving Mother that Christian parents must commend their children if they would wish to preserve them from the dangers that surround them. Oh! were God to lift the veil of futurity; could parents behold the lurking demons lying in wait to ruin their children, they would see the necessity of placing them under the special protection of the Blessed Mother of God. Teach the children to love Mary; teach them to be devout to Mary; teach them to pray to Mary, and to call upon her in every danger. Teach them expressly by word and example to love and to practise the holy devotion of the rosary and the scapular, which is so pleasing to Mary. Bequeath this devotion to them, and Mary will watch over them as a mother, and will guard them and guide them, until one day mother and child are united again in heaven.

St. Bridget had a son of the name of Charles, boyish alike in years and disposition. Having in his youth adopted the military profession, he soon met his death on the battle-field. The saint, reflecting on the dangerous time of life in which her son had died, the occasion, the place, and other circumstances of his death, was filled with great fear about his eternal lot. But God, who loved her tenderly, delayed not to comfort her by the following vision: She was led in spirit to the judgment-seat of the Eternal Judge, where she beheld, seated on a lofty throne, the Saviour Himself, with the Blessed Virgin, as Mother and Queen, at His side. No sooner had she appeared before the divine tribunal than Satan came forward, and, with a disappointed air, began boldly to speak as follows: " Thou, O Judge! art so right-eous in Thy decrees that I trust I shall obtain all I ask of Thee, even though I be Thine enemy, and though Thy Mother plead against me. Thy Mother wronged me in two points on the occasion of the death of Charles. The first is this: On the last day of the life of the young man, she entered his chamber, and remained there until he expired, driving me away, and keeping me far off, so that I was un-able to approach the bed and ply him with my temptations.

Now, this was a manifest injustice; for I have received a grant of the right to tempt men, especially in their last moments, on which depends the loss or gain of the souls which I so much long to make my own. Give orders, then, O just Judge ! that this soul return to his body, that I may have yet an opportunity of doing what I can, and of tempting him at least for the space of one day before he dies. If he resist courageously, let him go free ; if he yield to my efforts, he must remain under my power.

"The other wrong which I have suffered from Thy Mother is that when the soul of Charles had quitted the body, she took it in her arms, and herself brought it before Thy tribunal ; nor would she allow me to enter and lay my charges before Thee, although it is my office to prove the guilt of departed souls. The judgment pronounced was therefore invalid, for one of the parties remained unheard ; and this is against all the laws of God, and even of men."

The Blessed Virgin made reply to this complaint that, although Satan be the father of lies, yet on this occasion, speaking in presence of the Everlasting Truth, he had made a truthful statement, but that she had shown extraordinary favor to the soul of Charles because he had loved her tenderly, and had every day recommended himself to her protection ; because, too, he had always rejoiced when he thought of her greatness, and had ever been most ready to give his life for her honor.

In the end the divine Judge pronounced sentence as follows : " The Blessed Virgin rules in my kingdom, not as the other saints, but as my Mother, as Queen and Mistress ; and hence to her it is granted to dispense with general laws as often as there is a just cause. There was a most just reason for dispensing with the soul of Charles; for it was right that one who had in his lifetime so honored and loved her should be honored and favored in his death." Saying this, He imposed on the demon a perpetual silence as to this case. From this St. Bridget understood that her son had attained the bliss of Paradise.

Ah ! how truly does St. Alphonsus de Liguori assert that "the salvation of all depends upon preaching Mary, and confidence in her intercession." We know that St. Bernard of Sienna sanctified Italy; St. Dominic converted many provinces; St. Louis Bertrand, in all his sermons, never failed to exhort his hearers to practise devotion towards Mary; and many others have done the same.

Father Paul Segneri, the younger, a celebrated missionary, in every mission in which he was engaged, preached a sermon on devotion to Mary, and this he called his favorite sermon. The Redemptorist Fathers also have an invariable rule not to omit in their missions the sermon on Our Lady; and it is found that no discourse is so profitable to the people, or excites more compunction among them, than that on the power and mercy of Mary. To try to make the people good without inspiring them with love for the Blessed Virgin is to labor in vain. The better the people are made to understand what God has given us in Mary, the sooner they will lay aside their evil habits and practise virtue. For no sooner do they commence to love Mary and pray to her than they open their hearts to the largest channel of grace.

In the year 1835 the communions in a certain parish in the city of Paris, containing a population of twenty-seven thousand, did not exceed seven hundred. The good parish priest set to work to remedy this deplorable state of things; he formally placed the charge committed to him under the protection of Mary, and instituted her confraternity among his people. In the year 1837 the communions amounted to nine thousand five hundred; and each succeeding year they have become more numerous.

The spirit of infidelity and religious indifference is spreading rapidly in every direction. All the ills which an immoral and infidel press entails upon society, all the crimes arising from a godless education, menace the destruction of every vestige of Christian modesty, piety, and innocence Nothing better can be opposed to this infernal serpent than love and devotion towards her whose office it is to crush the serpent's head whenever it makes itself visible

Of all the sinners who, by favor of Our Lady, attained to an extraordinary degree of perfection, there was probably none more privileged than St. Mary of Egypt. It was through her devotion to Our Lady that she began, continued, and brought to a happy end the career of her perfection, and emerged from the abyss of degradation in which she lay to the sublimest heights of sanctity. Before her conversion she was a snare which entrapped every heart to enslave it to sin and to the devil; a net of which the devil made use to capture souls and to people hell. When the abbot St. Zosimus found her in the wilderness of Egypt, he requested her to give him an account of her life. This she gave in the following words:

"I ought to die with confusion and shame in telling you what I am; so horrible is the very mention of it that you will fly from me as from a serpent; your ears will not be able to bear the recital of the crimes of which I have been guilty. I will, however, relate to you my ignominy, begging of you to pray for me, that God may show me mercy in the day of His terrible judgment. My country is Egypt. When my father and mother were still living, at twelve years of age I went without their consent to Alexandria. I cannot think, without trembling, on the first steps by which I fell into sin, nor on my disorders which followed." She then described how she lived a public prostitute seventeen years, not for interest, but to gratify an unbridled lust; she added : " I continued my wicked course till the twenty-ninth year of my age, when, perceiving several persons making towards the sea, I enquired whither they were going, and I was told they were about to embark for the Holy Land, to celebrate at Jerusalem the feast of the Exalta tion of the glorious Cross of our Saviour. I embarked with them, looking only for fresh opportunities to continue my debauches, which I repeated both during the voyage and after my arrival at Jerusalem. On the day appointed for the festival, all going to church, I mixed with the crowd to get into the church where the holy cross was shown and exposed to the veneration of the faithful, but found myself withheld from entering the place by some secret but invisible force. This happening to me three or four times, I retired into a corner of the court, and began to consider with myself what this might proceed from, and, seriously reflecting that my criminal life might be the cause, I melted into tears. Beating, therefore, my sinful breast, with sighs and groans, I perceived above me a picture of the Mother of God. Fixing my eyes upon it, I addressed myself to that holy Virgin, begging of her, by her incomparable purity, to succor me, defiled with such a load of abominations, and to render my repentance the more acceptable to God. I besought her that I might be suffered to enter the church doors to behold the sacred wood of my redemption; promising from that moment to consecrate myself to God by a life of penance, taking her for my surety in this change of my heart. After this ardent prayer, I perceived in my soul a secret consolation under my grief; and attempting again to enter the church, I went up with ease into the very middle of it, and had the comfort to venerate the precious wood of the glorious cross which brings life to man. Considering, therefore, the incomprehensible mercy of God, and His readiness to receive sinners to repentance, I cast myself on the ground, and, after having kissed the pavement with tears, I arose and went to the picture of the Mother of God, whom I had made the witness and surety of my engagements and resolutions. Falling there on my knees before the image, I addressed my prayers to her, begging her intercession, and that she would be my guide. After my prayer I seemed to hear this voice : ' If thou goest beyond the Jordan, thou shalt there find rest and comfort.' Then, weeping and looking on the image, I begged of the holy Queen of the world that she would never abandon me. After these words I went out in haste, bought three loaves, and, asking the baker which was the gate of the city which led to the Jordan, I immediately took that road, and walked all the rest of the day, and at night arrived at the Church of St. John Baptist, on the banks of the river. There I paid my devotions to God, and received the precious Body of our Saviour Jesus Christ. Having eaten the one-half of one of my loaves, I slept all night on the ground. Next morning, recommending myself to the holy Virgin, I passed the Jordan, and from that time I have carefully shunned the meeting of any human creature."

Zosimus asked how long she had lived in that desert. "It is," said she, "as near as I can judge, forty-seven years." "And what have you lived upon all that time ? " replied Zosimus. " The loaves I took with me," answered she, " lasted me some time ; since that I have had no other food but what this wild and uncultivated solitude afforded me. My clothes being worn out, I suffered severely from the heat and cold." "And have you passed so many years," said the holy man, " without suffering much in your soul ?" She answered : " Your question makes me tremble by the very remembrance of my past dangers and conflicts, through the perverseness of my heart. Seventeen years I passed in most violent temptations and almost perpetual conflicts with my inordinate desires. I was tempted to regret the flesh and fish of Egypt, and the wines which I drank in the world to excess; whereas here I often could not have a drop of water to quench my thirst. Other desires made assaults on my mind ; but, weeping and striking my breast on those occasions, I called to mind the vows I had made under the protection of the Blessed Virgin, and begged her to obtain my deliverance from the affliction and danger of such thoughts. After long weeping and bruising my body with blows, I found myself suddenly enlightened and my mind restored to a perfect calm. Often the tyranny of my old passions seemed ready to drag me out of my desert ; at those times I threw myself on the ground and watered it with my tears, raising my heart continually to the Blessed Virgin till she procured me comfort; and she has never failed to show herself my faithful protectress." Zosimus taking notice that in her discourse with him she from time to time made use of Scripture phrases, asked her if she had ever applied herself to the study of the sacred books. Her answer was that she could not even read ; neither had she conversed nor seen any human creature since she came into the desert till that day that could teach her to read the Holy Scripture or read it to her; but " it is God," said she, " that teacheth man knowledge. Thus have I given you a full account of myself; keep what I have told you as an inviolable secret during my life, and allow me, the most miserable of sinners, a share in your prayers."

We can say that in the penitential life led by this saint in this solitude she had no other teacher, no other guide, than the all-holy, all-merciful Virgin, to whom she ever had recourse; it was under Mary's guidance that she overcame the most fearful temptations and withstood the most violent assaults that hell could make against her; faith in Mary triumphed over all feeling of weariness, trampled under foot the repugnance of poor weak nature, and enabled her to persevere constantly for forty-seven years, leaving to the world an ideal of perfect penance, a pattern of the most eminent sanctity, and a most convincing proof that there is no means more powerful than devotion to Mary to raise up any soul, however fallen and weighed down by sin, to the height of perfection.

A great power is evidently within our reach, placed by the care of God at our disposal, to assist us in our struggles against sin, to raise us when we fall, to carry us on to eminent perfection. It is easy of access; it lies at our door; it is within the instantaneous reach of all, even of children. That power is the influence of Mary and its employment in the work of our salvation. We may not reject its powerful assistance; nothing can be safely neglected that God has designed to make so perilous a work more sure. We may not throw away the aid thus offered, nor think to fight our way through the ranks of our spiritual foes without obligations to her, nor to speed on in our heavenward course without her helping hand. The heat of the battle will overcome us, the length of the way will exhaust us, unless she buoy up our steps and refresh us when we are weary. God's grace is free and strong ; but if she is the channel through which it must flow, it will not reach us but through her. We are not greater than Jesus, yet He made Himself her debtor; we are not stronger than He, and yet she was appointed to minister to His infantine weakness. Even if we could struggle through without her support, we should be outstripped in our course by many who started later and with many more disadvantages ; our passage would be joyless ; hope would shine dimly on the future.

What knowledge have we of the assaults of our spiritual enemies that may lie before us, perhaps in the hour of death. What security have we that if Mary does not assist us then, we shall not be lost ? It is for this reason that devotion to Mary is declared by eminent theologians to be a great sign of predestination, on account of the manifold assistance which is thus secured in its attainment.

In the *Chronicles of the Friars Minor* * we read that

* Lib. iv. cap. x rii.

Brother Leo, a familiar companion of St. Francis, had the following vision : The servant of God beheld himself placed on a sudden in the middle of a vast plain. There he beheld the judgment of Almighty God. Angels were flying to and fro, sounding their trumpets and gathering together countless multitudes of people. On this vast field he saw two high ladders, the one white, the other red, which reached from earth to the skies. At the top of the red ladder stood Jesus Christ with a countenance full of just indignation. On one of the steps, somewhat lower, stood the holy patriarch St. Francis, who cried aloud to his brethren on the plain below : " Come hither, brethren : come without fear; hasten to Christ, who is calling you." Encouraged by these words of their holy father, the religious crowded round the foot of the ladder, and began to mount. Some reached the third step, and others the tenth ; some advanced to the middle ; but all sooner or later lost their footing and fell wretchedly to the ground. St. Francis, beholding so deplorable a fall, turned to our Lord and earnestly besought Him to grant salvation to His children. But the Redeemer yielded not to the prayers of the saint. Then the holy patriarch went down to the bottom of the ladder, and said with great fervor, " Do not despair, brethren of mine ; run to the white ladder, and mount it with great courage. Fear not; by it you will enter into Paradise." Whilst he was thus speaking, the Blessed Virgin appeared at the top of the white ladder, crowned with glory and beaming with gentleness. And the friars, mounting the ladder by favor of Mary, made their way, and all happily entered into the glories of Paradise. We may learn from this how true is the sentiment of St. Ignatius the Martyr : " That the mercy of the Blessed Virgin Mary saves those whom God's justice does not save." Ah ! let us hearken to the words of this saint ; let us hearken to our Lord while He says to us from His throne in heaven : " I am tne eternal

222

Wisdom. I have come upon earth only through Mary; through her I have effected the redemption of mankind. If thou desirest wisdom and sanctity, call on Mary; for through her I will give it to thee." It was through her that Rupert the abbot, Albert the Great, Hermannus Contractus, and many others destitute of learning and talents became doctors in philosophy, theology, Holy Scripture, and other branches of science. "Thou art my child; I, therefore, am thy Father, but Mary is thy Mother. Thou art weak: I am the Lord, that giveth strength and help in all thy necessities.

"Thou art a sinful man, but I am thy God, full of love and mercy; Mary is the refuge of sinners, through whose mediation thou wilt obtain mercy. Thou aspirest after heaven; behold, I am the King of Heaven. Mary is the Queen of Heaven. In order to obtain for thee access to this heavenly kingdom, thou art bound to become holy. I am the living fountain of all grace, and holiness; but it is Mary who has the office of dispensing my graces. If thou, then, my child, desirest to obtain graces and glory in heaven, what hast thou to do? Call on Mary. Love and honor Mary. Through her I will listen to thy prayers and give ear to thy sighs. I will show her that I am her Son; and she will show thee that she is thy Mother. My Mother is the gate of heaven; through her all gifts and graces descend on earth; through her all the saints ascend to me into heaven.

"Accomplish, then, my will by endeavoring with all thy power to promote the honor of my Mother. Extol her at all times and in all places, in season and out of season; wherever thou art, praise and extol her, and cause others to do the same. Impossible for thee to give my Mother more honor, interior and exterior, than is her due. What is thy feeble love and honor compared to that which she receives from me? As thy love for thy fellow-men is but a shadow of my love for men, so thy special love for Mary is but a shadow, a faint, attenuated shadow, of my love for her ; for my sake, if thou wouldst please me, reverence her as much as thou canst. If thou hast hitherto served Mary, try to serve her still more fervently; if thou hast loved her, endeavor to love her still more ardently. Happy that Christian who serves Mary and at the same time tries to make others serve her ! Happy that Christian family in which Mary is truly honored; I will give it salvation and benediction. I will give it grace in the present life and glory in the life to come."

THE END.